W9-BYC-407

DISCARD

Augie's Quest

Augie's Quest

ONE MAN'S JOURNEY FROM SUCCESS TO SIGNIFICANCE

Augie Nieto

AND

T. R. Pearson

Foreword by Mitch Albom

BLOOMSBURY

Published by Bloomsbury USA, New York
Distributed to the trade by Holtzbrinck Publishers

All papers used by Bloomsbury USA are natural, recyclable
products made from wood grown in well-managed forests.
The manufacturing processes conform to the environmental
regulations of the country of origin.

LIBRARY OF CONGRESS CATALOGING-IN-PUBLICATION DATA
HAS BEEN APPLIED FOR.

ISBN-10: 1-59691-468-8
ISBN-13: 978-1-59691-468-1

First U.S. Edition 2007

1 3 5 7 9 10 8 6 4 2

Designed by Rachel Reiss

Typeset by Westchester Book Group
Printed in the United States of America by Quebecor World Fairfield

This book is dedicated
to Lynne,
my wife, soul mate, and the love of my life,
and to our four children,
Austin, Lindsay, Nicole, and Danielle.
I was drafted and they enlisted in this war.
I will be indebted to them for the rest of my life.

I also dedicate this book to the past, present, and future
sufferers of ALS. I will donate all proceeds from this book
to Augie's Quest.

All my love,
Augie

Contents

CONTENTS

Foreword

I NEVER KNEW the healthy Augie Nieto. By the time I was introduced to him, in his home in California, sitting in a chair, smiling broadly as he took my hand, he had already been diagnosed with ALS, and a transformation had begun.

By transformation, I do not mean the awful collapse the disease brings—the thievery of your walking, your lifting, your movement, your body. No. I refer here to the transformation of Augie's heart and spirit, its growth and full-scale blossoming. This happens sometimes with ALS, too. It happened with my old professor Morrie Schwartz. Similarly afflicted with this disease, Morrie observed, from a wheelchair, how leaves grow their most bright and colorful just before they die.

And he proceeded to do the same.

Augie Nieto is on that path. Although as successful as a man could ask to be, as wealthy, as handsome, as lucky in love and family as the mind can imagine, this, right now, is his shining hour. These days. This work. This book. This is his blossoming. ALS takes so much away. But in the right person, it also gives a great deal.

Augie is such a person.

He told me that day in his home by the sea that he was going to fight. He told me he was going to "beat this thing"—maybe not, to use baseball terms, in this inning, in this at bat, but before the end of the game. And I believe him. Anyone who talks to Augie believes him.

"I am blessed to have you as a friend," Augie has said to me many times, always, not surprisingly, beating me to the punch. Even slowed, Augie is quick. There is humor in his voice and whimsy in his eyes and a caring soul that exudes from his pores. You can understand how he built an exercise machine into a small business empire. You can understand why people flocked to work with him. He has a charm and a seductive inspiration. He would have made a great coach, because you are ready, after a half hour by his side, to knock down a wall for him.

And his gift to the world is his use of that inspiration in the fight against ALS. To my knowledge, Augie is the first person with this disease to employ business acumen to attack it. Eschewing the typical donation-to-existing-research approach, he has formulated a clear, multi-pronged plan for pulling up the roots of this disease. And he is charging at it with money, which means manpower, which means findings, which means progress, which means hope.

He does all this while still being the loving husband and father he has always been, while still finding time to laugh, read a book, shed a tear, or send encouraging messages to the many people who have contacted him.

During Morrie's final months, I witnessed him crying whenever he read about people suffering in the world, or saw footage of war on TV. I once asked him how he worked up such sympathy for people he'd never met in countries he'd never visited.

"When you realize your own mortality," he said, "you also feel the pain of anyone who's suffering. It doesn't matter where. We are all more alike than different."

I believe that is true. We are all more alike than different. That is the meaning of humanity. Augie Nieto appeals to the noblest part of that humanity, the bright, shining part of us, the part that wants to help others even as we need help ourselves.

He could have, years ago, written a book about his success in the business world. But he would tell you now, that would not have been his true story. This is his true story, and in it you'll find a piece of your own, a common nugget of humanity, a leaf of the brightest, most stunning colors. Augie Nieto has had many things taken from him, but what he has been given he shares now with all of us: the transformation of a heart that beats for itself to a heart that beats for the world.

—Mitch Albom,
author of *Tuesdays with Morrie*
and *For One More Day*

Get Your Affairs in Order

————◆————

THE TROUBLE BEGAN with a sharp twinge in the summer of 2004. Forty-six-year-old Augie Nieto had endured bouts of lumbar pain before, but this one was different, more tenacious and acute. The discomfort lasted for weeks and only ebbed after a full course of prednisone and three epidural injections. Augie attributed the ordeal to overexertion and middle age, but what seemed at the time an isolated episode would soon take on grimmer significance. That twinge would prove to be the opening salvo in a cascading calamity.

Over the course of the following months, Augie noticed a gradual erosion in his strength and endurance. A lifelong weight lifter, marathoner, and evangelical fitness fanatic, Augie was soon incapable of training with his customary hundred-pound weights. Then ninety pounds proved too much. Then eighty. And seventy. At length, he was reduced to working out with forty-pound weights, which he blamed largely on his weak back but also on the curious state of his right arm. The muscles had begun to twitch. The entire limb was alive, day and night, with rapid-fire, involuntary contractions. The condition was painless but maddening.

By early 2005, Augie's speech had slowed perceptibly, and he was having difficulty reaching across his body with his right hand to spread shaving cream on his left cheek. A January trip to Vietnam found Augie waterski-ing on the Mekong River, where the towrope pulled out of his hands, a novel experience for this veteran out-doorsman. "I'd never had that happen to me before," Augie confessed. "I came home and told my wife, 'We've got to check this out.'"

At the time Augie had no personal physician, but through the years he'd undergone numerous biannual executive physicals at the Mayo Clinic's Scottsdale facil-ity. When he called for an appointment, the staff was quick to accommodate him, and Augie and Lynne Nieto flew from their Southern California home to Arizona on the evening of March 23. The following morning, Augie met with the physician who would serve as coordinator and quarterback for the battery of tests he would undergo in the ensuing two days.

The Mayo Clinic prefers to start cold with its patients. Its doctors consult no past histories but begin anew with every evaluation. Augie merely provided a description of his symptoms, and a team of physicians—specialists in far-ranging fields—began quizzing and prodding him as they set about working with exhaustive deliberation toward a diagnosis. They analyzed Augie's blood chemistry, subjected him to thoroughgoing motor reflex tests, and performed both a CT scan and an MRI in a bid to pinpoint the cause of his degenerating strength.

Everyone hoped that the trouble would prove to be relatively benign, a case of heightened stress and overexertion or, possibly, chronic Lyme disease. But by Friday afternoon, Augie's team had only succeeded in eliminating potential culprits, not identifying a cause.

In a final meeting that day, a clinic neurologist asked Augie to stick out his tongue. "Thank God it's not vibrating," the doctor told him. "That's a symptom of ALS"— amyotrophic lateral sclerosis, otherwise known as Lou

Gehrig's disease. ALS remains incurable and is invariably fatal, typically within three to five years.

Augie passed along the news to his wife as they drove to the airport for their flight home. "They don't know what it is," he told her, "but at least it's not ALS."

Augie's lead physician had requested that he return to Scottsdale the following Monday. "You never," Augie quips these days, "want to get called back to the Mayo Clinic." Augie's younger brother Dave accompanied Augie and Lynne on this second trip. Doctors subjected Augie to an increasingly invasive series of neurological tests throughout the day. These culminated in an EMG, a procedure Augie never speaks of without wincing.

Electromyography, a nerve induction velocity test, requires the insertion of needle electrodes through the skin and into the muscles. The patient contracts and relaxes his muscles by turn, and the resulting electrical impulses register on an oscilloscope to be weighed against a known healthy standard. The disorders that can cause abnormal EMG results run into the dozens and include, in addition to ALS, Guillain-Barré syndrome and muscular dystrophy.

Most literature on the procedure includes language to the effect that the patient "may feel some pain or discomfort when the electrodes are inserted." Augie's description is a bit more incisive: "It hurt like hell."

Stretched out on the examination table, his body bristling with needles, Augie could see little of what was going on around him beyond the face of the neurologist conducting the test, who was monitoring the screen of the oscilloscope. "I was looking at the expression on his face," Augie said, "and it wasn't good."

By Monday evening, Augie still had no definitive diagnosis, though the inquiry was clearly moving into an area where none of the answers would be welcome. There is no affirmative test for ALS. The diagnosis is one of exclusion, and early Tuesday afternoon, Augie and Lynne entered neurologist Ben Smith's office and were confronted by some stark news. Augie's team of physicians had succeeded in eliminating all possibilities but two, multiple sclerosis and amyotrophic lateral sclerosis—MS and ALS.

A definitive test for MS requires a spinal tap—one more needle buried deep—which Augie submitted to later that afternoon. Then he, Lynne, and Dave awaited the results, passing several hours strolling through the Mayo Clinic's renowned cactus garden and indulging in what Augie and Lynne describe today as a perfectly surreal driving tour past Phoenix hotels for the benefit of Augie's brother, who was visiting the area for the first time. All the while, Augie and Lynne shared one wish. "Can you even imagine," Augie asks today, "hoping to have MS?"

By midafternoon on Tuesday, March 29, the spinal tap results were in, and Augie and Lynne sat together on Dr. Smith's office sofa awaiting Augie's diagnosis. Dr. Smith delivered the baleful news as delicately and empathetically as circumstances would allow. "I almost felt sorry for him," Lynne said, remembering that afternoon. "He was a very nice man, and very uncomfortable. I think I had tears running down my face. Augie was stunned. He didn't say a word."

Even after four rigorous days of testing at one of the premier medical facilities on the planet, Dr. Smith could only allow that Augie had an 80 percent chance of having ALS, a testament to the mysterious and elusive nature of the disease.

When Augie and Lynne asked about potential therapy and treatment, they got more bad news. There was only one FDA-approved drug specifically for ALS: riluzole, a glutamate blocker that can extend the life of an ALS sufferer by sixty to ninety days, though even those modest figures are in some doubt. "You'd best," Dr. Smith advised Augie, "get your affairs in order."

Lynne's Journal
April 4, 2005

It has been six days since we received the news—a nice doctor we had just met told us our lives would be forever changed. The world just stopped. I'm struggling with knowing that each day is a gift, and yet I've been unable to function. I feel dead inside. This is the first time I've been alone since the news. In some ways it's a relief but also terrifying. I can't stay on any task that doesn't involve cleaning—how stupid is that?

I have never felt so honest in my life, especially with Augie. I don't know how much time I have with him. For the first time in my life, I feel hopeless. Augie looks so sad and overwhelmed. I made myself read some of the material the doctor gave us—a booklet on "coping."

Scared, Sad, Disappointed, Unbelieving, Hopeless, Pathetic.

Osmosis

———◆———

ALS IS A motor neuron disease. Motor neurons are cells that move muscle. Upper motor neurons communicate impulses from the brain to the spinal cord, while lower motor neurons deliver those impulses from the spinal cord to the muscles.

If you bend to pick up a scrap of paper, a message of your intentions has traveled from your brain through a network of upper motor neurons to your spinal cord and out to the pertinent muscles that allow you to pivot and reach. ALS interferes in this process at the point where the lower motor neurons attach to the muscle, what is called the neuromuscular junction.

Affected neurons slowly die from the outside in. The location in the body where this cell death begins varies from person to person. Some cases of ALS originate in the vocal cords or the diaphragm. This type is called bulbar, and the degenerative progress of bulbar ALS is fiendishly swift. Patients usually die within one to two years of their initial symptoms.

More typically, the first symptoms of ALS appear as a weakness in one hand or one foot. In its earliest stages, this distal version of the disease is often misdiagnosed as carpal tunnel syndrome or dismissed as a pinched nerve. As the affected motor neurons begin to die, muscle activity becomes disregulated, and the muscles begin to twitch involuntarily. These sorts of spasms aren't uncommon in healthy people, but in ALS sufferers the twitching is unending and advances across the musculature of the body as the disease spreads.

While the onset of ALS manifests itself differently in different people, the progress of the disease is predictably radial. When symptoms begin in the right hand and arm, they will follow in the left hand and arm. Then the right leg, the left leg, and finally the torso. As more and more neurons die, the patient becomes paralyzed, trapped in an unresponsive body.

Commonly, ALS sufferers remain alert to their plight, and their brains go on working just as before, even if their bodies have abandoned them. ALS patients usually die either accidentally or intentionally—a ventilator fails or morphine doesn't.

•   •   •

NUMB AND DAZED, their lives changed irrevocably, Augie and Lynne returned to California after what they always speak of as *their* diagnosis. They summoned Augie's numerous siblings to their home. "We ate pizza, drank beer, and talked about anything but my disease," Augie said. The tone of the evening fit well with Augie's own response to the news: "I didn't deny I had ALS. I just didn't acknowledge it."

Augie found himself increasingly fixated on the seductive 20 percent chance that he'd been misdiagnosed.

Seven years earlier, Augie had seen his wife's case of granuloma, a readily treatable fishborne infection, get misdiagnosed, first as complex regional pain syndrome and then as rheumatoid arthritis, before a savvy physician finally identified the proper affliction. Hoping this sort of lightning might strike twice, Augie decided to seek a second opinion. He decided, in fact, to seek a covey of them.

Augie and Lynne enlisted Dr. Kent Bransford, Lynne's brother and a practicing oncologist. Though a trained physician, Kent required a quick education in the clinical details of ALS before he could be of much help to Augie. The disease is relatively rare, striking five thousand to seven thousand Americans a year, and Augie had already noticed—when informing his friends and family of his plight—that little was commonly known of the malady other than that it was invariably fatal.

Kent created an itinerary for Augie and Lynne to follow. He would travel as their neurological interpreter.

Augie carried with him the detailed results of his electromyography test at the Mayo Clinic. He'd decided one EMG in a lifetime was quite enough. Otherwise, he submitted to every procedure requested from UCLA at one end of the country to Johns Hopkins at the other. The diagnoses, seven in all, were depressingly uniform. No one ventured to contradict the Mayo Clinic finding. Augie Nieto had ALS. "It was incredibly demoralizing, getting the same diagnosis time and time again," Augie confessed. "I started to learn by osmosis that what they were saying to me is 'You're screwed.'"

Apparently, the process was so deflating that when Dr. Robert Miller, director of the Forbes Norris MDA/ALS Research Center in San Francisco, met Augie in his office and took an initial measure of the man, he sensed the depth of Augie's despair and immediately wrote a prescription for an antidepressant.

At that moment, Augie had plenty to be depressed about. Not only was he faced with the rigors of a degenerative disease of almost medieval nastiness, but his exposure to ALS experts nationwide had simply served to reinforce how little was known and settled about ALS.

Each specialist Augie, Lynne, and Kent met with seemed to have his own theory as to the root causes of the disease, and there was no unified thrust of research that appeared to promise a cure. Augie in particular came away from the trip with the sense that national research in the field was sorely wanting in the sort of creative thinking and open cooperation that might best result in effective treatment.

Augie returned to his Orange County home all but defeated and in a black frame of mind. A troop of ALS specialists had throttled his slim hope of a misdiagnosis while contributing little to no encouragement that Augie's affliction could be slowed in its dogged progress, let alone reversed. A mere eight months earlier, Augie had been the picture of health, and now he was in the grip of a disease that would rob him of his mobility, his voice, his breath, and eventually his life.

Augie and Lynne's house, an eccentric four-story structure, is perched dramatically above the Pacific Ocean on a rocky outcropping. Upon returning home with their diagnosis confirmed, Augie made a request of his wife with the surf breaking below him and a sweeping vista of Catalina Island before him. "Please," he implored Lynne, "let me die here."

Augie:

My right arm and leg were weak. My muscles were twitching. I hadn't gotten past the point where it was a nuisance, but I had the sense my muscles were disconnecting right before my eyes. I began feeling things that maybe weren't there. I became short of breath. I became unable to function without everything I did being colored by ALS.

I believed I had ninety days to live. I was experiencing each of the symptoms that were in the pamphlets, or at least imagining I was experiencing them. I couldn't help but jump to the worst.

Lynne:

He was out of it. He just wasn't there. He seemed like a small child, a body we just moved from place to place.

It *Is* About the Bike

———◆———

WHEN CONFRONTED WITH the news that Augie had been diagnosed with Lou Gehrig's disease, his friends and colleagues couldn't avoid the bitter irony of this turn in his life. Augie had long been a master of his circumstances, a paragon of fitness and a self-made businessman of impeccable credentials and enviable success.

Starting with little more than a salesman's instincts and a wealth of grit, Augie had built a thriving exercise-equipment empire. A popular trade publication famously referred to him as "the Henry Ford of the fitness industry." For this poor Mexican-Italian kid from Anaheim, the ascent had been remarkable.

Augie's father, Augustine, worked as a field foreman for Shell Oil and long struggled to provide for an ever-growing family. Augie was born on the fifteenth of February, 1958, a third son conceived after the second son, Bobby, had contracted leukemia. Bobby would die of the disease just before Augie's birth.

During Augie's early years, his mother served as a quiet, troubled presence in the family. Institutionalized on several occasions, Adele Nieto suffered from the lingering effects of the death of her second child. Augie's mother's despair reached a climax on the morning of her first son's graduation from college. She fixed a rope around her neck and hung herself in Augie's bedroom. Augie found her, barely alive. She died two days later.

So life grew even more challenging, especially for Augie, who, in addition to the loss of his mother and the stern ethic of his father, was battling his own demons. Augie was appreciably overweight, downright fat by his own assessment. At age fifteen, he was five feet six inches tall and weighed 260 pounds. His waist was forty inches around, and he was mercilessly teased by his schoolmates and effectively invisible to the girls in his class. To help remedy the situation, Augie embarked on a radical diet. "I ate nothing but watermelon for eight months. It was the one food that gave me cessation. I'd never had a cavity in my life but ended up with two root canals and six fillings. I did, however, go from 260 pounds to 158."

In addition to the watermelon, the weight loss was accomplished through devoted exercise. Augie ran day after day, mile upon mile, and he returned to high school for his junior year far different from the doughy kid his classmates had tormented the previous term. One student in particular was struck by the change. Lynne Bransford, now Lynne Nieto, noticed "this Mexican kid in the back of the room with a great laugh and a beautiful smile."

Augie and Lynne dated throughout their junior and senior years. "I was an auto-shop major in high school," Augie recalled. "Lynne told me I had to take chemistry and calculus. 'You're going to college,' she'd say. I was her project."

Upon graduation, Augie and Lynne made the amicable and sensible decision to break off their relationship while they attended separate colleges. Lynne was off to the University of California at Irvine, while Augie headed for Claremont Men's College, now Claremont McKenna College, a half hour east of Los Angeles.

Augie played football there. His coach, John Zinda, helped him land his first job on campus. Augie was charged with overseeing the weight room, and on his watch, virtually all the weights were stolen. Augie accepted full blame for the loss and responded by organizing a fund-raiser with his roommate, Scott McFarlane. The two could not have sprung from less-similar backgrounds. Scott's father was the CEO and founder of AIR-COA Hotel Partners, the largest independent hotel and resort management company in the world, while Augie was the son of an oil patch foreman of modest means.

Augie and Scott's initial business venture, a fund-raising jogathon inspired by embarrassed necessity, proved a staggering success. They raised $46,000 and managed to negotiate generous terms and favorable discounts with equipment suppliers by enrolling as wholesale distributors of their products for the Claremont area. Given the discounts involved, this tactic served to double the value of the money the two had collected.

"We figured if we really got behind this thing," Scott said, "we could sell the idea of this sort of fund-raising to high schools and colleges up and down California." The underclassmen called their business North American Stag as a tribute both to their university—the stag was the Claremont mascot—and to the breadth of their ambitions. Soon, though, the enterprise took a bit of a turn when several gym owners and athletic directors in Southern California asked Augie and Scott to supply them directly with discounted exercise equipment. So what had been North American Stag was reborn as North American Stag Fitness, and Augie and Scott began to function primarily as distributors.

The business had its own off-campus office and was owned and operated by the two full-time student athletes. Augie was the face of the company, the charmer and front man. "I was the guy," Scott recalled, "working in the back trying to take care of everything Augie was selling." And even as a college freshman, Augie proved an altogether remarkable salesman.

One of his storied triumphs involved a call Augie made on nearby Montclair High School. The stated purpose was to meet with a couple of coaches there to upgrade their school's gym equipment. "The next thing I knew," Scott said, "he'd talked them into being our partners in a fitness club. Both coaches took out second mortgages on their homes, quit their jobs, and we opened a gym right down the street from our office."

That gym would be the first of a string of successes for

Augie, a man who, according to Scott, could and would sell anything to anybody. Augie's caution-to-the-wind temerity was a direct result of his father's sacrifices. "When I started my own company, one thing I desperately wanted to do was take the biggest risk I could before I had a family. I had watched my father be trapped, and I was never going to let that happen to me. I didn't want to be my dad."

By Augie's sophomore year in college, his Claremont health club was a reliable going concern, but Augie was convinced he and Scott weren't squeezing all the potential profitability from the enterprise. The club was small by the standards of the time, only thirty-six hundred square feet, and had space for just one locker room, which meant that men and women were obliged to come on alternating days.

The gym floor was largely given over to Nautilus stations and other brands of weight lifting equipment. There was little cardiovascular machinery on offer at the time—just the odd primitive treadmill and decidedly unglamorous stationary bikes, chiefly clunky Schwinns and Monarchs.

Augie noticed the club's female membership was paltry compared with that of the men. Weight lifting at the time was almost entirely a male activity, so Augie was already casting around for female-friendly options when he encountered the device that would change not just his life but the face of fitness generally.

Augie spied his first Lifecycle—a revolutionary computerized stationary bike—in a fitness club in San Diego. The club was owned by a gentleman named Ray Wilson, who had purchased the North American rights to the bike. What most excited Augie was clear evidence of enthusiastic use of the cycle by women in Wilson's club. Wilson had four Lifecycles on the floor of his gym, and all of them were very much in demand by the female membership. What Augie didn't know was that Wilson owned ten Lifecycles at the time, but due to their poor reliability, he could only manage to keep four operating at once.

The original Lifecycle was invented in 1968 by Keene Dimick—an overweight Canadian chemist who'd designed and built the bike in a bid to get himself into passable shape. Dimick had made attempts through the years to interest American fitness entrepreneurs in his cycle, but he was early on the scene. The word *aerobics* had only been coined in the late sixties by Air Force physician Kenneth Cooper, and Jim Fixx's seminal book on the

benefits of aerobic exercise, chiefly in the form of jogging, wouldn't be published until 1977. Dimick's Lifecycle
was programmed to take its rider through a series of
simulated hills and valleys as a means of elevating and
decreasing heart rate by turn. The ride lasted precisely
twelve minutes, and the rider's progress was charted on a
rudimentary screen with illuminated red dots.

The Lifecycle wasn't much to look at. Even Augie had
to confess, "It was incredibly ugly." Nonetheless, he saw
extraordinary potential in the bike. It held the promise of
making the health club experience far more attractive to
women and thereby tapping into an entirely new customer base that had gone unserved by the general re-
liance on free weights and weight machines. "A club with
both Nautilus and Lifecycle," Augie decided, "would have
the complete package."

Augie negotiated his way into a distribution partnership with Wilson, who, given his ratio of broken Lifecycles to sound ones, was pleased to share the burden of
marketing such an erratic contraption. Augie sold his interest in the Claremont fitness club to the two former
high school coaches, and he and Scott threw in together
on a secondhand RV, fondly named Sluggo, which would
serve as their national Lifecycle sales fleet.

They equipped the vehicle with a bike for demonstration purposes and went touring around the country, visiting trade shows and fitness clubs. The fact that the bike was reliably unreliable didn't even figure into the troubles Augie and Scott confronted on that initial sales trip.

The type of cardio fitness machine the Lifecycle represented was relatively new on the scene, and many of the gym and health club owners were devoted muscle heads—lifelong weight lifters and Nautilus advocates who didn't share Augie's hunger for the coming cardio wave. Worse still, Augie and Scott were buying the units for two thousand dollars and selling them for three thousand dollars. The wholesale price of the competing Monarch stationary bike was only six hundred dollars.

Over the next nine months, even sales phenom Augie could only manage to move eleven Lifecycles. "I was four hundred thousand dollars in debt," he said, remembering those days. "I would have declared bankruptcy if I hadn't owed all the money to my friends and family."

What had been a string of successes for North American Stag Fitness came to an abrupt halt. It seemed a good time for Scott to reconsider his prospects. "I was going into the family business," he said, "and since we didn't know where any of this was going, me and Augie just kind of drifted apart." Optimistically, Augie had ordered nearly three hundred Lifecycles, which he was storing in an Irvine, California, warehouse. In a moment of daft brilliance, he decided to start giving them away.

"I told my partner, Ray Wilson," Augie recounted, "that we could leave the bikes in the warehouse as the best-kept secret around, or we could give away fifty bikes and let the club owners have a chance to use them in their homes." So Augie selected fifty club owners from the scores of men he'd met during his tour in Sluggo and shipped them each, at no charge and with no obligation, one spanking new Lifecycle.

In return, Augie Nieto absorbed a valuable lesson in human psychology. "I learned a very important thing," he says now. "Reciprocity. Once you give somebody something, they owe you."

The orders began to trickle and then gush in. Even though Augie had greased the wheels with free Lifecycles, the price of the bikes remained a thorny issue, so he leased the bikes on generous terms and thereby leveled the ground with competitors. In 1979, the price of a Lifecycle was seventy dollars per month per bike, and the machine was such a novelty that gym owners were able to charge their members an extra fifty dollars a year for the privilege of using one. In 1979, eleven Lifecycles were sold and fifty were given away. By 1980, the company could boast half a million dollars in sales, though not to entirely happy customers. The relatively delicate nature of the machines was becoming apparent. "The Lifecycle had issues. It didn't work very well," said Bryan Andrus, who was destined (or doomed) to a thoroughgoing acquaintance with every troublesome Lifecycle component.

Andrus had met Augie in Claremont. He'd been working part-time at a racquet club when Augie and Scott called him in to give advice about the design of their fitness center. Like Augie, Andrus had been immediately and instinctively open to the potential of the Lifecycle. "I'd seen what it did for people, what happened to them when they got on it," he said. All that was left was for young Bryan to explain to his parents why he was dropping out of Pitzer College to work for a guy selling exercise bikes at four times the going price.

"My parents told me," Andrus recounted, "'We don't remember dropping you on your head when you were a child.'"

BRYAN ANDRUS:

Health clubs are a hell of a business model. They're a little like HBO—high up-front cost, and people pay to be able to access them. But unlike HBO, people have to get up off the couch, get in their cars, drive to the gym, and pay for the privilege of submitting themselves to personal hardship.

AUGIE:

My philosophy is to never think your customers have no options.

Sprint and Recover

——◆——

B RYAN ANDRUS JOINED Ron Dorwart in the Irvine plant where the Lifecyles were assembled and, almost invariably, disassembled as well. Dorwart, a Canadian Lifecycle enthusiast, had traveled to Irvine in 1977 hoping to work on the bike. "I think I only got hired because I had a truck," Dorwart recalled. "I didn't even fill out an application. My first day, I was getting five dollars an hour, and I drove down to San Diego to fix a Lifecycle." In those days, according to Andrus, "once you put a Lifecycle together, you were pretty much guaranteed to be taking it apart again, probably counted in weeks."

Augie kept selling the bikes and guaranteeing them.

"With Augie, everything was a guarantee," according to Dorwart. "That's how he made his name. He'd replace a bike, no questions asked, and they'd buy ten more." Augie was wedded to the principle that it was far wiser to keep an old customer than to have to troll for a new one, so he promised to repair or replace every bike sold. That proved a rather expensive promise to keep with the first few editions of the Lifecycle. "I sold them," Augie said. "Ron built them. And Bryan fixed them, and boy was Bryan busy."

The challenge lay in building a sufficient quantity of Lifecycles to keep up with growing demand while correcting the numerous design flaws that prevented the bike from performing robustly in a gym setting. Dorwart ran down the litany of weak actors: "brake arms, pedals, mechanical drives, electronics, you name it." The Lifecycles were getting used and abused to an extent that Augie and his crew hadn't really anticipated and probably couldn't have addressed but for fortunate timing and happy accidents. "Plastic membranes came out along about then, so we could use that. And there were all kinds of side innovations in electronics, in plastics, in switch and ancillary stuff that we were able to take advantage of," Andrus said. "A year earlier, and we'd have been sitting around with our schlontzes in our hands saying, 'How are we going to fix this?'"

Ron Hemelgarn, the owner and operator of a string of health clubs in the Midwest, was one of Augie's first customers. In the early 1980s, Hemelgarn owned upward of two thousand Lifecycles, so he was well acquainted with both the lure of the device and its welter of problems. "I had spread Lifecycles into my clubs throughout the country," Hemelgarn remembered, "and I'm getting phone calls about these bikes breaking. In some clubs we'd even sold memberships to use the Lifecycle, so we had a real fiasco on our hands. I was pretty upset, and I had Augie come out to my office in Toledo. I said, 'Augie, this is crazy. I've got all of these bikes and they're breaking. Our members are irate. What are you going to do?'"

"He gave me this white cardboard box with red and blue lettering on it," Hemelgarn recalled. "It read, 'Instant Service Kit.' I opened it up, and here's a handlebar and a seat, different tools for adjustments, different things. I was mad because I'd spent a lot of money to buy this junk, but I looked at that stuff and had to laugh. I recently found out that mine was the only kit they'd made. That was just to pacify old Ron who'd bought all these bikes."

Instead of losing a customer, Augie endeared one to

him. "Augie was a young guy with a lot of drive and a lot of determination. When you shook his hand, it was a deal," Hemelgarn observed. "That's not only rare in this business, it's rare in industry generally."

Hemelgarn stayed with Augie and stayed with the Lifecycle. By his reckoning, he's probably the oldest continual customer the company has. "From those early errors and problems, they made a great, reliable product. And that's what matters."

In 1985, Bally Manufacturing (now Bally Technologies) came courting, and Augie and his partner, Ray Wilson, sold Lifecycle Inc. for ten million dollars. Augie stayed on to run the company, which was soon renamed Life Fitness, and the business continued to grow and prosper. In 1990, Augie partnered with Mancuso and Company, a New York–based banking firm, to buy the company back. By this time, Life Fitness boasted annual revenues of eighty million dollars.

Augie continued to be the face of the company. His handsome mug appeared regularly in promotional material for Life Fitness products, and Augie functioned as an inspiring testament to the transformational power of exercise. The fitness industry loved him because his Lifecycle wasn't merely profitable for Life Fitness but was bringing members into clubs around the country and across the globe.

Though Life Fitness was ever expanding and sales continued to grow at a steady clip, Augie's business style remained unchanged from the early Lifecycle Inc. days. Augie continued to operate by handshake rather than contract, and his personal mantra for all business dealings was "Underpromise and overdeliver."

Life Fitness now had offices in Asia and Europe, so there was always business to be conducted, no matter the hour, and Augie's preoccupation with the health of his company all but eclipsed the meager interest he'd reserved for the rest of his life. He had married his college sweetheart, Karin Fitzpatrick, in 1984, and during this period, Augie was largely ignoring not just his wife but his entire family. His son, Austin, had been born in January of 1986 and his daughter, Lindsay, in February of 1989. Augie's regular business hours began most days at six in the morning and continued until near midnight. As CEO and joint owner of Life Fitness, he was consumed with the company's success to the decided detriment of his home life.

In May of 1992, Augie returned to his home one evening to find his clothes neatly packed in a suitcase and his wife intent upon his departure. Augie moved into a nearby Residence Inn. "I thought I'd be asked back," he said. "Nineteen months later, I caught on."

Augie took the occasion of his separation and eventual divorce to reflect on how he had been living. "As good as my business life was, my home life was nonexistent. For the first time," he said, "I realized I needed to be a complete person myself, that no one else could complete me." Augie embarked upon a course of therapy with the goal of arriving at a better understanding of not just himself but his children too.

Therapy helped Augie understand that he wasn't always obliged to be productive. In describing his breakthrough, Augie likens life to a marathon: "If you never allow yourself to have a finish line, you end up plodding along forever, when we all need to sprint and recover. Recovery is sleep. Recovery is laughter. Recovery is spending time with your kids. I learned to sprint and recover."

Augie was jarred and lastingly changed by the breakup of his marriage. It touched every part of his life. "Up until that point," he said, "I had never failed at anything I did." According to Augie, the crisis taught him the fundamental value of embracing risk. "The worst that can happen is that you'll have an opportunity to learn. I'd never thought that before."

At work he became a different creature and was quick to acquaint his employees with his new appreciation for setting finish lines, for sprinting and recovering, what Augie chose to call the "ideal performance state." He actively encouraged his employees to take their vacations, enjoy their families, and leave work at work. This was a new worldview for Augie, who took his own advice and lavished attention on his children, while setting clear boundaries between working hours and leisure hours. He began to look at life not just as an earning opportunity but as something to relish.

Around this time, in early 1994, Augie answered a phone call from Lynne Bransford, his high school sweetheart. Lynne had married in 1980 but had recently separated from her husband, and she was calling to work Augie for a deal on exercise equipment for an apartment complex she owned and managed.

The Augie Nieto on the other end of the line in 1994 was not the same man Lynne had known a decade earlier. The old Augie had been, in Lynne's view, "a bit of a jerk." The new Augie impressed Lynne immediately as more thoughtful, kinder, far softer around the edges than the man she remembered. The two embarked on a long-range courtship between Chicago, where Augie was living, and Southern

California, and the high school sweethearts were finally married in the summer of 1995.

Augie considered the combination of reacquainting with Lynne and his full embrace of the "ideal performance state" a kind of double-barreled epiphany. He was personally content, and Life Fitness was booming along as successfully as ever. Augie was patriarch of a large and happy blended family—Lynne had brought two daughters, Nicole and Danielle, to the marriage—and on those occasions when he relapsed into compulsive behavior, the object of his compulsion was almost invariably recreation rather than work.

One spot of the breakneck variety very nearly crippled him in 1997. "I was on a snowmobile trip to Finland, and I was out of control," Augie admitted. Along on the trip was Bryan Andrus, Augie's old friend and product engineer from the early Lifecycle days. The two men shared a snowmobile, with Augie at the controls, and they were traveling in the windswept wastes north of the Arctic Circle when near tragedy occurred.

Augie was motoring along with the throttle wide open when he lost control of the snowmobile and managed to collide squarely with what Andrus described as probably the only tree at that latitude. Andrus estimated they were traveling better than thirty-five miles an hour. "Augie was my air bag," he said, before recounting a dreamlike climb out of the swale they had veered into. At the crest of the adjacent hill, Andrus gazed down at the wrecked snowmobile and the man crumpled beside it. Thoroughly dazed, he wondered aloud, "Who's that?"

Augie lost consciousness briefly, but he soon came around to discover he'd not been so lucky as Andrus. The collision had shattered his left knee. He was in agony and incapable of standing, which presented a grave problem for Augie and his companions since they were several miles from the nearest road and hours from the closest hospital.

The conditions were so inhospitable and frigid as to argue against leaving Augie and venturing out to seek help, so Andrus applied his engineering skills to the construction of a rude sled. The thing was tethered to the rear of a snowmobile, and once Augie had been gingerly placed upon it, the party made the two-hour return trek to the road.

A radio call brought Finnish police to the scene, and the officers insisted Augie submit to a Breathalyzer test. They were reading the results when Augie told them, "Nope. This was all me."

He was then transported to Lapland Central Hospital

in Rovaniemi, where Augie made a call to Lynne to tell her what had happened. "I was expecting a loving wife on the phone," Augie said, but the news of Augie's wreck and the admission that his heedlessness was the cause of it put Lynne in a less than sympathetic mood. "You don't have the right," she told him, "to drive a snowmobile into a tree with the five of us behind you."

Augie was stunned by Lynne's tone and by her words, but he took occasion to be enlightened as well. "That was probably the first time," Augie insists today, "I truly understood that it's not all about me."

Lynne's Journal
April 13, 2005

Augie has been speaking such kind words of love and caring to me, and I seem to be tongue-tied. I'm trying hard to take his words in, to digest their meaning, to remember them long into the future when he can no longer speak to me, when he can no longer hold me in his arms. Our friends and family will return to their own lives after the dust settles. Will my memories be enough?

Finding Bottom

———◆———

B Y MAY OF 2005, nearly two months after his diagnosis, Augie had yielded to depression tinged with denial. "I had this disease, but I was trying to convince myself it wasn't going to affect my life," he said. He was determined to believe he'd been afflicted with what Lynne now sarcastically calls "the kinder, gentler ALS."

Augie soon found that, unless he was medicated, anxiety would keep him awake most nights, so he began to dose himself with Ambien nightly in combination with an antidepressant that complicated his despair rather than relieved it. "The medicine made my heart race and left my mind foggy," Augie recalled. "I'd never taken an antidepressant before, and I was fearful of my family history, of the issue with my mother."

During these weeks, Augie "wasn't even present," according to Lynne. "He'd almost ceased to function." Given his circumstances, Augie's reaction was hardly surprising. Here was a man who'd spent the bulk of his life devoted to fitness, not just personally but professionally, and he now found himself in the clutches of a disease that was sure to deprive him of control over the body he'd worked to create.

Moreover, the great luxury of wealth and the consolation of possessions had largely been swept away by Augie's diagnosis. His funds would guarantee him the best care available, but there was no cure to be bought at any price, only various ameliorating treatments.

ALS is a ruthless leveler, and since his diagnosis, Augie had done little but sink. He was pharmaceutically addled and nearly paralyzed by depression. Nothing seemed worth doing, worth savoring, worth hoping for, and by Memorial Day of 2005, Augie had reached bottom. "I woke up in the middle of the night," he said, "and I was on the dark side."

"I'd decided I didn't want to impose my disease on my family," Augie said, so he rolled out of bed and went into the bathroom. "I think I took eight pills, and I didn't wake up the next morning." He had choked down a fistful of antidepressants.

Augie hadn't plotted to kill himself. He insists it had never so much as crossed his mind until he awoke in the small hours of Memorial Day. "I thought I was okay when I went around the country visiting the doctors," Augie said, "but when the trips were over, I had to deal with the reality of the disease. I really don't even remember what I did. It was nothing planned. I woke up in a cold sweat, and all I wanted to do was escape. I wanted Lynne to be able to get on with her life without having this anchor around her neck. I was suddenly damaged goods and felt she didn't deserve it. I took the easy way out."

When Lynne awoke on Memorial Day morning, she found Augie still asleep beside her. "But nothing looked right," she said. "Augie was snoring loudly, which wasn't normal. When I nudged him to turn him over, he didn't move. Then I shoved him, and I shook him, and he still didn't move." That was when Lynne spied an empty pill bottle on the nightstand, a bottle she knew had been nearly full just the day before.

Lynne called 911 and rode in the ambulance with Augie to nearby Hoag Hospital. The doctors on duty were soon convinced that Augie's life wasn't in immediate danger, but he'd taken enough drugs to leave himself comatose, and he was admitted to the hospital, where he would stay for the next four days.

He was put on suicide watch, which meant a nurse remained at his side, day and night. Lynne moved into the room as well and slept on a cot while she waited for Augie to regain consciousness.

Lynne had decided to tell few of Augie's friends and family members about his condition and the reason for it. One of Augie's oldest buddies and his colleague at Lifecycle, Peter Brown, happened to be visiting at the time, and Lynne called on him for support. She also told Augie's children from his first marriage—his daughter, Lindsay, and his son, Austin—precisely what their father had done.

"At the hospital, even though I seemed unconscious and couldn't talk," Augie recalled, "I was able to hear most of what was said in my room. I heard my wife and my kids and my brothers and sisters talking, and they didn't know I could hear them. I had the surreal experience of being at my own memorial service and watching and hearing what people were saying."

Though Augie wouldn't regain full consciousness until

late Tuesday, he had enough brief lucid moments before then to permit Lynne to assure him that, if he truly wanted to die, she would find a way to help him. Though Augie's doctor told Lynne that Augie's life was never in legitimate danger, Lynne's physician brother, Kent, remains convinced that Augie's was "a genuine suicide attempt."

When Augie finally awoke on Wednesday to find his family gathered around him, he exhibited the blend of remorse, shame, and deep sorrow befitting a man who'd never intended to open his eyes again.

"I was embarrassed," Augie said. "I remember snippets of people who came in—my kids, my wife, my brother and sister—and I had this revelation that I should be incredibly proud of having a wife and children, a family that wanted me around. If they could love me like they did, I was going to do everything I could to earn back their respect."

Augie would be in the hospital another full day. By then he'd already sweated most of the drugs out of his system and had decided that he would do without his sleep aid and his antidepressant from that point forward, that he would face his plight unmedicated and grapple with it as best he could. Augie was discharged on Thursday,

June 2, with the cause of his stay at Hoag Hospital still a guarded secret. So while he had amends to make and apologies to deliver, they were far fewer in number than they might have been.

Once back at home, he sat his daughter and son down at the small table off the kitchen that had lately become his work space. "The hardest conversation I had was with Austin and Lindsay," Augie said. "I told them I was sorry for what I'd done to them. Austin said, 'You were my hero and now I don't have the same level of respect for you.' It was at that moment I said, 'I'm going to earn it back.'"

Austin was openly angry with his father. "My sense of how to be a good person," he said, "a good man, had come from my father. I thought he took the easy way out. He kept saying he didn't want to be a burden on us, and I told him, 'Are you kidding me? I'd walk through hell for you.'"

Austin readily admitted that he'd had a shallow relationship with his dad before the onset of ALS. They worked out together, lifting weights usually, and they talked like a couple of guys working out. But once Augie's symptoms had taken hold and an afternoon in the gym was out of the question, Austin and Augie were obliged to find another way to be, and they discovered a bond well beyond exercise.

The two are joined now at what Austin is quick to call "a new level." Austin can understand and appreciate the man who'd feared he would become a burden to his family, and Augie can understand the rage of a son who'd resented that fear.

Augie emerged from Hoag Hospital still an ALS patient but an entirely different man. "For the first time," Augie said of those initial hours and days following his overdose, "I accepted the disease. And once you accept it, you're back in control."

DAVID MALCOLM—a friend of Augie and
Lynne's from the Young Presidents' Organization,
a private assembly of business titans with chapters
across the globe:

*Rob Rodin and I came up with the idea of confronting Augie
shortly after his diagnosis. Augie wasn't being Augie. He was in
denial about his disease, so Rob and I decided to set up an evening
where we could spend some time together with Lynne and Augie
and talk to Augie about dealing with the issues facing him.*

*We ended up having a pajama party on Augie and Lynne's
boat. We brought six pairs of pajamas, and Lynne and Augie, Rob
and Debbie Rodin, me and my wife, Annie, were all in silk pajamas having dinner, drinking wine, and laughing.*

*Afterward, Augie led Rob and me to the upper deck and took
off his shirt. All we could see was his body twitching. I couldn't believe my eyes and asked him, "What's happening?" Augie explained that his muscles were detaching and ALS would slowly
rob him of his ability to breathe.*

*We then confronted him about how he was going to deal
with his diagnosis. It was Rob who finally said to him, "You've*

been very successful, but how will you use this disease to become significant?"

Until recently, I didn't know Augie tried to commit suicide the very next day.

AUGIE:

When I finally woke up in the hospital, I knew what I had to do. It was like throwing a light switch. I felt acceptance—of my symptoms, of my disease—and I felt back in control. I was no longer reacting but was able to act.

Once again, I felt I could be the one who could define the rules and make the game I wanted. In acceptance, I found the capacity to let others help. I could be vulnerable, which made me more approachable, and I allowed people back into my life.

LYNNE:

A much-humbler Augie came out of the hospital. I think there was an awful lot of remorse. The day he came home, Augie was determined to tell Austin and Lindsay everything he needed to tell them about how to live their lives.

It seemed as if he was trying to come to grips with what had happened. He was unconscious for almost two days and was frail, but he was clearly grateful to be alive.

AUGIE:

I felt a complete change in temperament. I could now think through how to take my newfound acceptance and put it into action.

No Way to Run a Business

———————◆———————

I N CONSIDERING HIS visit to the dark side, Augie decided, "If that's the worst, everything else is better. I
was no longer fearful, fearful of the progress of the disease, fearful of the knowledge of whether I was loved and
respected." The Augie Nieto who returned home from
Hoag Hospital was very different from the man who'd
wandered into his bathroom in the small hours of Memorial Day morning to choke down a fistful of pills. Lynne
noticed the change immediately. "Augie started looking
forward," she said.

He was back home by the first week in June and already anticipating the planned renewal of his and

Lynne's vows on the anniversary of their marriage. The service was scheduled for later that month, and family and friends who attended saw a renewed Augie, a determined and optimistic Augie, reaffirm his love for his wife of ten years.

During this same period, he was also occupied with a constructive look back. He was only then beginning to digest all the details of his experience traveling the country visiting clinics and doctors devoted to ALS research and treatment. He had been in such an inky funk at the time, a state of psychological shock, that he'd barely been capable of putting one foot in front of the other.

Upon reflection, Augie realized he'd come away with a distinct sense of how unsettled and outright contradictory much of the clinical perspective on ALS tended to be. In reviewing what he'd been told specifically and the literature that had been passed along to him, Augie became aware of how little was known about the disease he had.

No one could say with any certainty whether sporadic ALS, Augie's type, was genetically based or environmentally induced. Approaches to treatment varied from specialist to specialist, and Augie noticed the pronounced isolation of the neurologists from each other. "Everybody," Augie remarked, "was working in a silo."

Historically, ALS research has been conducted by scientists and doctors attached to universities with grant funding supplied by the National Institutes of Health and various nonprofit organizations, led by the Muscular Dystrophy Association. Given the rareness of the disease, the competition for dollars, and the relatively low level of ALS funding ($42 million projected for 2007 for ALS research, as compared to $1 billion for Alzheimer's and $4.6 billion for cancer), these studies are prone to be modest in scope, and pharmaceutical companies can't be bothered to invest their considerable research dollars in a disease that has only five thousand to seven thousand new cases annually.

By this time, Augie was fully awake to the complications of his disease and had shed denial in favor of an appetite for every scrap of ALS-related information he could come by. "I became a student of the research," Augie said of that time, "and I found that institutional, academic researchers were under an incredible amount of pressure to generate a novel hypothesis and then prove its validity." Unfortunately, Augie's silo analogy was all too apt. Scientific findings rarely if ever traveled from one university institution to another in an efficient, informal way. Occasionaly, peer-reviewed papers were presented at professional gatherings, but the process struck Augie as overly formalized and far too deliberate.

The trouble at bottom, as best as Augie could tell, was a strain of academic contamination. The researchers were highly protective of their studies and their data and cultivated a counterproductive isolation for what impressed Augie as petty reasons. The old joke goes that quarrels between academics are so fierce because the stakes are so small. In Augie's view, here were researchers engaged in matters of life and death for Augie and his fellow ALS sufferers who were failing to treat the stakes with the urgency they deserved. They were behaving more like academics than healers.

A frequent observation of Augie's is that a "system is incapable of viewing itself," so sometimes the most astute assessments are made by people coming from the outside. At the time, Augie may have been an ALS neophyte, but he was an old and highly successful hand in the corporate world. His observation of the leading ALS clinics and their maddening lack of interplay and organized oversight had led him to one concrete conclusion: "That's no way to run a business."

◆　◆　◆

PART OF AUGIE'S education in the neurological intricacies of ALS and the general state of play in drug therapy and ALS treatment came in the form of a seminar he and Lynne attended at an Orange County hotel in the summer of 2005. The session was conducted by Jamie Heywood, whose younger brother, Stephen, had been diagnosed with ALS in December of 1998.

Jamie's response to his brother's illness had been to learn everything he could about ALS and the therapies available. His reaction to what he discovered had been much like Augie's. Jamie found research on the disease to be piecemeal and appallingly slow, fundamentally due to ALS's orphan status as a disease with a national prevalence of around thirty thousand cases annually. Moreover, the general approach to solving the considerable neurological puzzle presented by ALS impressed Jamie as far too conservative to produce the sorts of near-term results that might help his brother.

In response, Jamie and a couple of friends—none of them with medical training—started the ALS Therapy Development Foundation in his basement. The object was to engage in what Jamie called "guerilla research" and thereby revolutionize the stodgy traditional approach to ALS therapy. The plan initially was to raise enough money to fund cutting-edge research, but given the general paucity of it, the ALS Therapy Development Foundation eventually opened a laboratory of its own.

The foundation took space in a Cambridge, Massachusetts, warehouse district and started its own mouse lab with the intention of testing every approved pharmaceutical agent available that might have even an accidental effect on the degenerative progress of ALS. The foundation was canvassing for a drug without bothering to develop a theory of ALS and its causes first, an approach bluntly antithetical to the academic method.

The creatures employed in such tests, called SOD1 mice, are genetically engineered with a human gene that gives them a form of ALS. Their symptoms are much more compacted than those exhibited in people. The mice generally lose their ability to walk after ninety days and die in four or five months. The mice are also fairly pricey at upwards of seventy-five dollars an animal, before housing and testing are factored into the equation, which raises the price per mouse to nearly two thousand dollars. So the ALS Therapy Development Foundation, in funding its own laboratory, needed to bring in cash at a healthy clip to keep ahead of the cost of operations.

To that end, Jamie traveled the country delivering his ALS 101 seminars and soliciting donations. The session Augie attended lasted the better part of an afternoon and had drawn the friends and families of ALS sufferers, along with several ALS patients. Jamie gave a layman's account of the medical history of ALS and described the slow, degenerative progress of the disease in language the audience could readily understand.

Augie responded instinctively to Jamie's passion for his mission. Jamie was after nothing less than an outright cure for ALS and some therapeutic means of reversing the ravages of the disease. The prevailing view among physicians, as voiced by Lynne's oncologist brother Kent, tends to be less ambitious. "With ALS, the hope is to revert it to a chronic disease," Kent said. "I think of it as a parallel with cancer, where we can treat some cancers and get people back to normal." He went on to add, however, that "to reverse the effects of ALS, you're almost faced with having to reconstitute the nervous system."

In pursuing a cure, Jamie had done everything within reason to bring the plight of his brother to the attention of the nation. With the exception of Mitch Albom's sociology professor, Morrie Schwartz, no ALS sufferer was more widely known than Jamie's brother, Stephen Heywood.

Stephen and Jamie were featured in a *New Yorker* profile, and their circumstances were presented at exhaustive length in a book by Jonathan Weiner, *His Brother's Keeper*. Additionally, at the time of Jamie's L.A. seminar, the family had been living under the scrutiny of a pair of filmmakers for a couple of years. The result would be *So Much So Fast*, a documentary devoted to the travails of Stephen's disease and to the heroic efforts of the volunteers and employees at Jamie's ALS Therapy Development Foundation to find a cure.

What Augie detected in Jamie was the power of single-minded devotion, not all of it harnessed to best effect. As a businessman—and more pertinently, as the CEO of a successful manufacturing concern—Augie had developed a nose for efficiency. So while he admired Jamie's tireless commitment to his stricken brother and applauded his ambitions, Augie couldn't altogether endorse the foundation's scattershot approach to fund-raising, which appeared to leave Jamie scrambling for cash to keep the operation afloat.

"I saw how great the science was," Augie said of the foundation, "but I found the fund-raising more a matter of happenstance and not well disciplined."

Like Jamie, Augie wanted to find a cure for ALS, and he was growing increasingly aware that the effort would require a monumental amount of money and an entirely new way of thinking about medical research. Augie, ever the entrepreneur, found himself entertaining the notion of replacing the traditional academic research model with an industrial one. Work would be efficient and speedy; data would be openly shared; potential drug targets would be licensed for profit to pharmaceutical companies.

The man widely known as the Henry Ford of the fitness industry was, by grim necessity, considering a new career.

AUGIE:

I saw my first ALS patient at Jamie's seminar. He was in a wheelchair in the back of the room. All I could see was his chair. All I could hear was his respirator.

LYNNE:

I remember that. It was like . . . holy shit! That's ALS.

Hookers and Muffins

———◆———

THE NATIONAL PREVALENCE of ALS—the total number of cases at a given point in time—hovers around thirty thousand. Consequently, not many people in the country—certainly no one in the government—wake up every morning determined to find a cure for this relatively rare disease.

Only the Centers for Disease Control approaches medical problems with anything like the urgency Augie had hoped to discover among ALS researchers. Sean Scott, current president of the ALS Therapy Development Institute in Cambridge, describes the predicament this way:

SARS rolls into the country. Some red light goes off at the CDC, and everybody puts on the monkey suits, and bang, it's time to go. They were sending people to Asia. They were shutting down airports. They were developing diagnostic assays. They were screening drugs against the virus. Because it's an infectious agent, and infectious agents can wipe out whole civilizations. The government is completely aligned to take care of that kind of thing. But if it's an existing disease, the question to pose is, Why treat it any differently? It might not be a crisis for you, but it's a crisis for me.

In Sean's case, the argument is more than rhetorical. His mother died of familial ALS, and Sean calculates his own chances of contracting the disease as "a coin toss."

So Augie wasn't alone in his frustrations, but who was this exercise guy to tell anybody in the field of ALS research what to do and how to do it?

Even early on, before he'd come to grips with his diagnosis, Augie had begun to wonder if the quest for a cure for ALS wasn't simply a business problem awaiting a solution. What he couldn't have known at that moment, when his frustration was greatest, was that he had an ally in his timing. Augie needed a cutting-edge plan for the money he intended to raise. Sean needed a pile of money for the cutting-edge plan he'd developed.

At that time, late spring of 2005, Sean was head of research and development for what was then called the ALS Therapy Development Foundation, the organization started by Jamie Heywood in Cambridge. Sean is neither a physician nor a trained scientist. He is, rather, a former filmmaker with a degree in rhetoric from the University of California at Berkeley. An inspired amateur, that is to say, in the field of ALS research, very much like Augie Nieto.

ALS runs in Sean's family on his mother's side. The affliction is known as "the family curse," and in the late nineteenth century it claimed five of Sean's grandmother's eight siblings. Sean's mother's initial symptom presented in February of 2000, when she was fifty-seven years old. Her voice elevated an octave. "My mom was first diagnosed with asthma," Sean recalled. "We were doing our best to make it be something else."

Once the proper diagnosis could no longer be avoided, Sean sat down with his stepfather, and they divided up the duties at hand. "I said, 'You make her comfortable, and I'll go out and make sure there's no stone unturned.'" Sean visited the University of California at San Francisco medical bookstore and collected every pertinent neurological textbook he could lay his hands on. "I bought three or four thousand dollars' worth of books at once," Sean said. "They looked at me like I was insane."

Once home, Sean sat down with one of the books and was stumped the third word in. "I'd had the foresight to buy a medical dictionary," he recalled, "and I looked up the definition, but then I had to look up every word in the definition. It was just a flat-out war of attrition."

Over the next couple months, Sean plowed through his textbooks. "I did a PhD program's worth of reading," he said, and he came away with a full and troubled appreciation of ALS research. "The bad news was that nobody had any idea what was going on with the disease," Sean said. "The good news was I was on an even playing field. My ignorance at the time was state of the art."

In scouring the Internet for any lead on potential ALS treatment, Sean came across the ALS Therapy Development Foundation. From his San Francisco apartment, he began to communicate with Jamie Heywood and other members of his team, which had been organized initially—following Jamie's brother's diagnosis—to raise money for ALS research and distribute it to best effect.

Jamie and his colleagues had soon realized what Sean Scott and Augie Nieto discovered independently. Academic ALS research, the only strain of scientific inquiry available, seemed to lack the velocity and sense of dire purpose that Jamie demanded for his brother, that Sean required for his mother, that Augie needed for himself.

Spurred by unsatisfying options in the research field, the team at the ALS Therapy Development Foundation decided to set up a research program of their own, the laboratory in which they would test the available worldwide pharmacopoeia on genetically engineered mice. The intent wasn't simply to run drugs approved for the treatment of ALS through rigorous animal studies, but to test every drug on offer, the global FDA catalog, for potential effect in slowing the disease or reversing its damage.

Most drug compounds operate in ways that are mysterious to the companies that produce them and the doctors who prescribe them. The vast majority falls into the category of "dirty" drugs. They perform the task they've been developed to perform but perform countless collateral tasks as well. "Most drugs you run on a gene chip will move a thousand genes," according to Sean. "Take a drug like Claritin. It moves a thousand genes. So it's all well and good it's an antihistamine, but it also may be a cure for cancer."

The prevailing thinking at the ALS Therapy Development Foundation was that one or more of these dirty drugs might affect the progress of ALS on a cellular or even genetic level in such a way as to provide useful therapy or indicate a fresh lead in understanding the disease. Sean—timing again—had discovered the foundation just as the mouse lab was becoming a reality. The foundation's new approach tacitly acknowledged what Sean had found out on his own: nobody knows anything.

Sean volunteered to help in any way he could and so shifted, in essence, from tracking down a treatment for his mother to pursuing an outright cure for her disease. "Because I'm a megalomaniac," Sean confessed, "I went from being in charge on behalf of my family to being in charge for thirty thousand people."

Sean worked for free for months. "I was watching my bank balance drop like a thermometer in Alaska," he said. Finally he enlisted help from his uncle. "He stepped up and donated enough so that I could draw a salary and bought me time to get my arms around the problem." Sean's uncle is Edward W. Scott Jr., a Silicon Valley tech pioneer who forged great success in the 1990s as cofounder and president of BEA Systems.

In 2000, when he first made contact with the ALS Therapy Development Foundation, Sean was all of thirty years old. While he had no formal medical training, his grasp of the encyclopedic intricacies of ALS in particular and neuropharmacology generally—after two months of solitary reading—confirmed him as a remarkable autodidact. Sean could speak with a scientist's informed authority on ALS, and this from a man who, prior to his mother's diagnosis, worked as a successful director of Bay Area television commercials.

Sean quickly ascended the ranks to run the entire research operation in Cambridge. "Every meeting with pharmaceutical companies has this moment we've all come to enjoy," said Fernando Vieira, one of Sean's comrades in the lab. "Sean will lay out, in painful detail, the hurdles associated with spinal drug delivery and neuropharmacology for ALS, and invariably they'll ask him where he trained. When Sean answers 'CBS' they go white."

Upon graduating from college in 1991, Sean had gone into business with his father, Richard Scott, and his girlfriend, Nancy Kelly. The three had bought a struggling video postproduction company in San Francisco, and they specialized in making video inserts for news broadcasts and television commercials for the local market.

When Sean discovered the ALS Therapy Development Foundation, the organization was in need of someone with his eccentric skills. The new laboratory had a supply of SOD1 mice, creatures engineered to mimic ALS, as well as several technicians and pharmaceutical scientists. What they didn't have was ready, affordable access to a stream of drugs for testing. That's where Sean came in.

"Acquiring drugs and working in the film industry," Sean said, "are pretty much the same thing." In his nine-year career as a director of TV commercials, Sean had developed a knack for getting whatever he needed—equipment, permits, props—when he needed it.

"In the movie business," Sean insisted, "there's no problem that can't be solved with hookers or muffins." The pharmaceutical business was different but apparently not different enough to prevent Sean from finding a way to procure the drugs his scientists wanted to test at the best possible rates.

The ALS Therapy Development Foundation had no one in charge of business development in the early days of the mouse-screening program. "Frequently a scientist would say something like 'I wish we had this Pfizer drug,'" Sean recalled. "When I asked them why they didn't get it, they'd tell me companies didn't give that stuff out. So we just started picking up the phone and asking for drugs."

Sean had enlisted Nancy Kelly's help. "If being in the film industry prepares you for anything," Nancy said, "it's getting stuff for free and getting it fast." By combining chutzpah with sheer relentlessness, Sean and Nancy soon established over fifty corporate collaborations and opened a worldwide supply line of pharmacies across Europe and in Israel, Asia, Africa, and South America.

Sean and Nancy would order the drugs needed for testing, and if they couldn't get them domestically, one of their foreign pharmacists would fill the order and ship it to Puerto Rico. From there the orders traveled by mail to Boston.

"I never envisioned myself a drug runner," Sean said, "with suppliers and mules on five continents trafficking in pharmaceuticals, but these were desperate times." The drugs in question were dispensed legally all over the world, but many were not yet approved for domestic use.

The object was to run the compounds through a series of tests on the lab's genetically engineered mice to see what, if any, effect they might have on the rapid progression of the mouse version of ALS.

Where familial ALS is concerned, the laboratory realized dramatic success. The cause of familial ALS, compared with the sporadic strain, is rather straightforward. The disease is triggered by a misshapen protein, SOD1, that's normally a harmless antioxidant. "That misshapen protein exposes a kind of sticky residue that cakes up in places," according to Sean. "The argument starts when you ask, 'What part of this mechanism is this protein screwing up?' My contention would be it's screwing up between ten and one hundred factors simultaneously, and getting rid of the protein is the only way of going after the disease."

The fundamental difference between self-taught Sean Scott and a trained neuroscientist can be seen in Sean's unwillingness to tease out the cause behind the misshapen protein and the specific ways in which that deformity may trigger disease. "The actual argument about what it does," Sean insisted, "is academic and not very productive."

The goal, in Sean's view, is simply to decrease the

level of SOD1 in the body substantially. "If a kid lights a building on fire," Sean asked, "do you chase him or grab a hose?"

◆   ◆   ◆

SEAN'S MOTHER DIED in October of 2003. "It was a twenty-four-hour-a-day fight that he thought he could win; we all did," said Nancy. "The end for her was ugly. Her disease was so aggressive, she couldn't even blink."

In mid-2004, one of Sean's cousins was diagnosed with familial ALS. By this time Sean's group in Cambridge had been screening drugs for three and a half years with very little success. "I was starting to think we were banging our heads against the wall," said Sean. "My cousin's diagnosis was a wake-up call for me. The defect in this protein was found in the midnineties, and nobody had bothered to develop a drug to get rid of it. It's a simple concept—less protein equals less disease."

Since there was no drug currently identified that had the ability to lower the offending SOD1 protein, Sean realized one would need to be found or built. The Cambridge lab was not designed for this purpose. "This was a different kind of science done almost exclusively by drug companies," said Sean. "I thought, if you can't get a drug company to build us a drug, let's build a drug company."

Sean was able to cobble together enough private money, largely from his uncle Edward and other family members, to get a drug development company off the ground. Alsgen started with a bang, discovering a drug that lowered levels of the offending SOD1 protein within five months of opening its doors in Monmouth Junction, New Jersey.

The drug was pyrimethamine, already FDA approved. It had been used for years, chiefly in Africa, as a synthetic antimalarial. As a collateral effect, it reduced SOD1. Sean's cousin was the first patient to take it. His symptoms were already well advanced, and the drug seemed to have little effect. The next five test patients, also far into their disease, showed no improvement as well.

Then came encouraging results from a couple of early-stage patients. One of them, frighteningly enough, was yet another cousin of Sean's. Progression of the disease in both patients was arrested for an extended period, upward of fourteen months—a revolutionary result in the treatment of ALS.

Sean won't let himself get too excited. "Even though a stoppage of disease is rare in familial ALS patients, we can't know how significant this is until we've seen it in a lot of people."

Of Alsgen, Augie said, "This business model is critical. We need to shift the financial burden to the private sector as soon as we have a validated target. This strategy is a big part of beating sporadic ALS as well. The perception by drug companies that ALS isn't a profitable disease is just wrong, and many of them don't know it yet."

Augie's contention is based on a case study of a drug called Ceredase, a treatment for Gaucher's disease, a rare malady caused by an enzyme deficiency. Made by Genzyme Corporation, Ceredase grosses close to a billion dollars a year with a client base of only 2,300 patients. The key to the profitability of drugs like Ceredase is the 1983 Orphan Drug Act, which legislates distinct market advantages for companies willing to develop drug therapies for those diseases that affect fewer than two hundred thousand Americans in a given year.

One such advantage is that there's no limit on pricing for drugs designed to treat an orphan disease. "With a client base of over thirty thousand people," Augie said, "there's eighteen billion dollars in available revenue for ALS." The Genzyme model involves charging close to $180,000 per year per patient. "Genzyme has an insurance claims group," Augie added, "that simply deals with reimbursement for patients. If the patients don't have insurance, Genzyme donates the drug and writes it off."

Whether it's getting women to come to the gym or drug companies to come to the table, it's all the same to Augie. "Available market drives everything," he said. "That gives us the leverage to fund the construction of a real drug. Eighteen billion dollars is a major market prize. The question is, Who's going to get there first?"

AUGIE:

I had to explain the disease to most people. That was pretty awkward. They just didn't know what it was. I'd say 95 percent of the people we'd see had heard of ALS but knew nothing of the course of it.

I remember when I first saw my neurologist, he told me, "The good news is you're going to live longer than the average ALS patient. The bad news is you're going to live longer than the average ALS patient." I didn't even know what he was talking about.

The Luckiest Man
on the Face of the Earth

———◆———

W HAT MOST AMERICANS know of amyotrophic
        lateral sclerosis, they learned at the movies, in-
structed by one of this nation's most celebrated sufferers,
Gary Cooper. Cooper, of course, merely played the role
of Lou Gehrig in *The Pride of the Yankees,* but Cooper's version of Gehrig's stunningly selfless speech before thousands of fans in the Bronx ranks in the top ten of the
American Film Institute's favorite movie moments.

If pressed on the nature of Gehrig's affliction, most film
fans specifically and Americans generally would likely
respond that Gehrig had ... you know ... Lou Gehrig's
disease.

In this instance, our collective ignorance when it comes to amyotrophic lateral sclerosis is probably less the result of habitual American know-nothingness and more in the way of a sad reflection of the intricate, neurological mystery that is ALS. Gehrig's circumstances are reminiscent of Augie Nieto's, only played out on a larger canvas.

Gehrig, like Augie, was a physical specimen whose career depended on his fitness and athletic prowess. Born in 1903 in New York City, Gehrig attended Columbia University on a football scholarship. He was six feet tall, a large man for his day, and when he began to play baseball for the Columbia nine, he immediately captured the notice of big-league scout Paul Krichell, who signed him to the Yankees in 1923.

Gehrig played most of that year with the Hartford farm team but was called up to the Bronx in September, where he made an impression with a gaudy .423 batting average in twenty-six at bats. During the 1925 season, he replaced Wally Pipp at first base for the Yankees, and Gehrig would field his position—game in and game out, year in and year out—without missing a single contest for the next thirteen years.

During the 1938 season, Gehrig's production fell off

considerably in September after a blistering August when he batted .400. By season's end, he was hitting weak fly outs instead of home runs. His batting average had dropped to .295, and his stamina had quite obviously begun to flag. By spring training of 1939, the deterioration of Gehrig's skills was conspicuous. He had a difficult time fielding even the gentlest ground balls and was prone to lurch about the infield.

On opening day, 1939, Gehrig fielded first base and continued at the position for the ensuing seven games. He proved ineffective, however, as a hitter and was such an embarrassment in the field that he pulled himself from the lineup. After fourteen years and over two thousand consecutive games, Lou Gehrig's professional baseball career was over. He was thirty-six years old.

Encouraged by Yankees president Edward Barrow, Gehrig scheduled a checkup at the Mayo Clinic in Rochester, Minnesota, and submitted to six days of testing in June of 1939.

Once an official diagnosis had been made, the Mayo Clinic issued a press release at Gehrig's request. His illness was identified as ALS, which was described in the release as a disease that "involves the motor pathways and cells of the central nervous system and in lay terms is known as a form of chronic poliomyelitis (infantile paralysis)."

ALS, of course, is not a form of polio, and it is acute rather than chronic. The common belief, reinforced by the clinic's press release, is that Gehrig's team of Mayo physicians never fully informed their patient of his prognosis. Lou Gehrig seemed to think he had a fifty-fifty chance of recovery on a course of vitamin therapy.

On July 4, the Yankees held "Lou Gehrig Appreciation Day" at the stadium in the Bronx. Gehrig approached a microphone at home plate and told the assembled fans and teammates, his amplified voice echoing through the stadium, "Today I consider myself the luckiest man on the face of the earth." The film version, cloyingly romantic, ends with Gary Cooper striding into the Yankee dugout. In truth, Gehrig's struggles were only beginning.

As a national figure, Gehrig served to focus public attention on ALS and spark a popular spike of interest in ALS research, but the vitamins he was taking (vitamin C and niacin, primarily) had no effect on the disease, and he degenerated steadily.

Lou Gehrig died in his Bronx home on June 2, 1941, two years after his diagnosis and two weeks shy of his thirty-eighth birthday.

While Lou Gehrig's "bad break," as he chose to call it, brought ALS to the American public's attention, it was by no means a new malady at the time of Gehrig's diagnosis. The disease was first described by French physician Jean-Martin Charcot in 1874.

Charcot was able to observe the progression of the disease in one of his chamber maids, and he authored the first exhaustive description of the malady he named amyotrophic lateral sclerosis. *Amyotrophic* is Greek for "no muscle nourishment." *Lateral* identifies the area of the spine damaged by the disease, and *sclerosis*, or hardening, refers to the nature of that damage.

What Charcot observed in the steady degeneration of his maid was a sort of wasting disease that gradually compromised the voluntary muscles throughout the body but had little to no effect on involuntary muscle function. The heart continued to beat. Bladder and bowels performed normally. Eye-muscle reflex was unaffected, as was sexual function. The disease also seemed to have no adverse bearing on the five senses—touch, taste, smell, hearing, and sight.

The disease left mental faculties unimpaired as well, so Charcot's maid remained cruelly alert to her predicament as her body grew increasingly nonresponsive. The spread was distal at first. She lost the use of her arms, then her legs. Her speech slowed and thickened as prelude to utter silence, and her breathing became increasingly labored once the deadening effects of ALS had spread through her trunk to her diaphragm.

As was dependably the case in Charcot's day, his maid died of slow, inevitable suffocation. The disease had run its course in slightly over three years.

Charcot could be almost as certain of the cause of the disease as neurologists are today, which is to say not certain at all. The factors that visit ALS on one person but spare the next are frustratingly elusive. The root causes of the malady are possibly environmental, perhaps viral, conceivably genetic, probably all in erratic combination.

ALS presents in two distinct forms, one of which is passed genetically through families. Familial ALS, Sean Scott's mother's strain, constitutes little more than 2 percent of the overall instances of the disease. What is called sporadic ALS makes up the balance. While the symptoms are similar to identical in both strains, the cause of familial ALS is known to reside in the interplay between a specific mutated enzyme and an inherited genetic disposition.

Cases of sporadic ALS, on the other hand, seem to spring from a myriad of potential causes in jumbled combination.

Suspected triggers include toxins, viruses, infections, and inflammations. The most commonly held theories on the genesis of sporadic ALS propose that any or all of these factors may combine catastrophically with un-scripted genetic variations, called polymorphisms, to touch off the disease.

There have been odd spikes of ALS incidence in cor-ners of the world, one occurring in the eastern Pacific, where residents of the Kii Peninsula of Japan exhibited a susceptibility to the disease one hundred times greater than normal, the cause of which remains a mystery.

In Guam, natives were also contracting ALS at an alarming rate due to what researchers decided was a pre-vailing island appetite for the cycad seed. The cycad is a widely distributed palmlike plant that produces a natural nerve toxin. The natives of Guam processed the seeds into flour and regularly ate bats that fed on cycad seeds and had accumulated the toxin in their flesh. Once local officials had prevailed upon the natives to alter their diet, the incidence of ALS fell dramatically.

There are documented cases of ALS developing in the wake of electrical shocks and after prolonged contact with agricultural pesticides. Several studies have revealed a higher-than-average incidence of ALS among veterans of the Gulf War and their spouses. And mysterious clusters of the disease have been identified in San Antonio, Texas—thirty-nine cases among current and former employees of Kelly Air Force Base—and in western Connecticut, where Lyme disease has been floated as a possible trigger.

Professional athletes have long been cursed with a heightened disposition for ALS. Bone-breaking trauma has been implicated as a factor in the disease. In the course of one particularly unlucky stretch, three San Francisco 49ers players from the 1964 team were diagnosed with ALS, visited in trio with an affliction that normally affects one out of every one hundred thousand U.S. citizens.

In the United States, the commonly accepted statistic for ALS incidence is five to seven thousand new cases per year. Determining the true number of cases is complicated by the diagnostic difficulties ALS presents. Many patients exhibit symptoms one to three years before they are properly diagnosed.

Neurologist Stanley Appel, a highly regarded ALS specialist who operates a clinic at the Methodist Hospital in

Houston, often refers to ALS as the nice guy's disease. "The likelihood of a nervous, perturbed patient having ALS is pretty slim," Dr. Appel said. His far-ranging experience—he sees a majority of the ALS patients in the eastern United States and sits on the board of the Muscular Dystrophy Association—has led him to conclude that most people stricken with the disease are selfless and compassionate. Dr. Appel isn't entirely sure if the patients started this way or if ALS-induced changes in the brain have sweetened already-genial dispositions.

As an illustration, Dr. Appel told the story of a patient he diagnosed, a gentleman typical of what Dr. Appel called "the nice guy phenotype." The man was a former football player and a quarterback coach at Texas A&M. When Dr. Appel told him it looked like he had ALS, the coach and his wife wept, and they were shortly joined by Dr. Appel. "We carry around boxes of Kleenex here," he said of his clinic. With his neurologist still crying before him, the coach drew himself to his full 6'4" height, laid a hand on Dr. Appel's shoulder, and said, "It must be tough telling patients they have ALS."

Dr. Appel remains remarkably sanguine about the chances of developing a cure for ALS, while acknowledging the idiosyncrasies of the disease and the challenges they present. "There's even the issue," he said, "of whether ALS is a single disease—absolutely identical in every patient. It could be differently caused or initiated in different people." There's certainly no argument that the disease progresses differently from patient to patient.

Generally, the younger the onset, the slower-moving the disease, and the older the onset, the faster-moving. Dr. Appel refers to ALS as "a disease of older age." But while the median age of ALS onset is fifty-seven, he recently saw an eighty-eight-year-old patient with early symptoms of the disease, and he has treated more than a few twenty-somethings with ALS.

In Dr. Appel's opinion, the disease is probably touched off by a combination of "environmental factors and genetic susceptibility factors." He is particularly suspicious of the role of inflammation in the development of ALS. "We think the immune cells are fundamentally dictating what is happening to the motor neurons," he said. But he's also quick to allow that the "natural history of ALS might be changing."

In reference to the abundant theories about the causes of ALS, Dr. Appel suspects that everyone is right. "There are probably various factors that affect the energy factories of the cells," he said. These might include environmental toxins, viruses, infections, and physical insults such as bone trauma, all in combination with one or more susceptible genetic variations.

In his multidisciplinary Houston clinic, Dr. Appel both treats his patients and provides them with access to the latest technology in wheelchairs, communication devices, and ventilators. Though there's no known cure for ALS just yet, or even an effective means of slowing the progress of the disease, Dr. Appel and his fellow neurologists can address many of the collateral issues that arise for ALS patients. Drugs exist to control the physical side effects—increased saliva, phlegm in the lungs, bladder spasticity—and to regulate the emotional upset that generally attends the disease.

Beyond that, Dr. Appel openly traffics in optimism. "You can't cure them," he allowed of his patients, "but you can give them a sense of hope, which will prolong their lives."

Dr. Appel confesses to being high on the potential of stem cell research in combination with genetic profiling to lead the way toward a cure for ALS. Furthermore, he is convinced that the portions of the lower motor neurons affected by the disease at the neuron-muscle junction can be regrown, promising a complete reversal of the debilitating effects of ALS.

For the moment, however, Dr. Appel and his colleagues are chiefly obliged to deal in hope. And if Stanley Appel's patients are grateful for his compassionate care, he seems equally appreciative of the chance to provide it.

"I think doctors who take care of patients with ALS have a unique privilege," Dr. Appel insisted. "The patients give us more back than we ever give them, in terms of affection and meeting people's needs. From a scientific point of view, you almost have a chance to see the brain in solo flight."

CHIP BAIRD—founder of North Castle Partners, a leading equity firm:

When Augie first joined North Castle as an advisor, we had a retreat that was a combination of business and social activities.

One of the first events was meant to be an icebreaker. We'd hired a martial arts instructor to teach yoga and stretching and take us out of our comfort zone. It was meant to be a curveball and catch people a little off guard.

As the session started, we were all balancing on one leg, but Augie was having nothing to do with it. He sat down, leaned against the wall, and said something like "Who does this guy think he is. He's offered us no objectives, no milestones, no agenda. What is he trying to do?"

That was classic Augie. If he wasn't "the man," if he wasn't in control, he was having no part of it. At that time, Augie only played by his rules, and he wasn't really able to see other perspectives. It was his world, and we were just passing through it.

I visited Augie recently, just the two of us at his house. Augie was confined to his chair, and I saw a man who'd become a distilled, high-powered problem solver. Augie was focusing his brain on a series of business and people problems. He was sensitive, attentive, empathetic, giving—a new Augie.

On the one hand, his transformation struck me as incredibly sad, and yet Augie came across like a prophet operating on a different plane.

A Molecular Fishing Expedition

———◆———

B Y LATE SUMMER of 2005, Sean Scott had overseen
his lab's rigorous review of every major ALS drug
study coming out of academia. There had been eighty-
one of them over the course of five years, the majority
funded by the National Institutes of Health. The ALS Therapy Development Foundation in Cambridge had established that none of the drugs tested in these studies had
prolonged the lives of the lab's genetically engineered mice.

The results fueled an internal debate over whether the
mice were treatable at all. There was also the starker likelihood that the mice were treatable but the drugs simply
didn't work. That would mean, after many years and

much NIH funding, that the pursuit of a cure for ALS was exactly where it had started. At zero.

So it was a blend of frustration and burgeoning desperation that prompted Sean to pick up the phone one day and introduce himself to Sharon Hesterlee, the vice president of translational research at the Muscular Dystrophy Association. The MDA is the largest nongovernmental supporter of ALS research in the country. Of its $35 million annual research budget, around $7 million goes to ALS research, and the organization supports the most extensive network of ALS clinics in the nation. The MDA had ALS patients who needed drugs, and Sean and his lab, though empty-handed at the moment, were devoted to developing drug leads in need of human testing.

Sharon holds a PhD in neuroscience. She started her career as a bench scientist but soon discovered she had no taste for lab work. "It's too much like cooking," she said, "just adding ingredients all day long. I loved science, but I didn't like the process of doing it." That realization led to a job as a science writer for the Muscular Dystrophy Association, which she held until she got "hijacked by the research department."

Sharon is in the habit of scouring the scientific landscape for new and innovative ideas the MDA might put some funding behind, and Sean's phone call came at an opportune moment. Sharon had recently been reflecting on the grants awarded by the MDA and the NIH in the ALS arena and had wondered if both organizations were spending their ALS funding as wisely as they could.

Sharon and Sean discovered they had similar ideas about the course and nature of ALS research. Sharon saw in Sean's lab a program organized around the notion that testing could and should be speedy, efficient, and thorough. The foundation, Sharon recognized, "had been running drugs at a huge scale and volume, much more than any academic lab had done."

Moreover, Sean's laboratory had repeated experiments that had already been published. "Their results were all negative," Sharon remarked, "which didn't win them any friends in the academic sphere." Sean acknowledged "hurt pride" among many academic scientists. "I think they thought we were making them look bad," he said.

Sean just wanted something that worked, "and it wasn't out there," he said. Sharon was coming to the same conclusion, and she and Sean began to discuss an entirely new approach to ALS research. "We did an exhaustive review of clinical trials," Sharon recalled, "and we really hit the wall. We needed to step back and take a fresh look at this disease. It was clear there was something important about ALS we didn't understand."

Sharon and Sean agreed it was time to start over with ALS research. "We should just surrender," Sean proposed. "We have no idea what's going on in sporadic ALS. Let's just look at this every way we can and see what data falls out."

They were proposing to dismantle the disease on a molecular level, to approach it unarmed with theories or scientific preconceptions. They would treat ALS like it was new to the earth and start fresh with all of the tools at their disposal. Theirs would be a sort of fishing expedition. As Sharon said, "If you want to catch fish, go fishing."

The research plan hatched discreetly between the two of them was revolutionary, a strain of scientific pipe dream. To become a reality, their plan would need vision, relentless drive, and an enormous amount of money. Sean's calculations ran toward sixty million dollars.

◆　◆　◆

AUGIE'S GENERAL EXASPERATION with the state and pace of ALS research and drug development had come to mirror Sean's frustration with ongoing scientific results at the ALS Therapy Development Foundation.

The sheer volume of data generated by the foundation's mouse trials had inspired Sean to develop what he called "pipeline" software. "At the time, there was no way to come into a disease space and ascertain everything that had come before," Sean said, so he'd written a program that allowed the foundation to categorize worldwide research on ALS and record new leads in drug therapies around the world.

Sean's software served as a kind of global disease radar. He and his team at the foundation could now track every emerging therapy from every lab on the planet. The team had a professional "treatment investigator," who kept constant tabs on ALS clinics and the patient community to determine if anything of therapeutic value was emerging.

This was exactly the kind of informed overview Augie had found lacking in the academic ALS research model. Sean insisted that researchers generally, and ALS researchers specifically, needed to be aware of all therapies in development before they could best judge how to spend their time, energy, and precious funding.

"If you walk into a disease space with a big wallet and

an itch to solve a problem," Sean said, "you probably can't even get a list of what's been tried before, let alone what worked, what failed, and what's likely to have promise. All that's available are press releases generated by universities to pump up interest in funding their projects."

Sean's software was born of necessity. "We needed to know where to put our muscle," he said. "There's no sense in working on something that's already failed several times, but that happens every day in the silo system."

On his own, Augie had sensed the dire need for a schematic of the ALS landscape. "Trying to attack a disease this complicated without a comprehensive map," Augie had grown to believe, "is like trying to run an air war after the radar screens go black."

Sluggish pacing and poor coordination weren't the only problems with ALS research, however. There was also an enormous development gap when it came to ALS drug therapies. "Academia isn't doing anything wrong necessarily," Sean said. "They're doing what their programs were built to do," which he identifies as "descriptive biology." The trouble is that academia has a feeble record of creating drugs.

In 2006, the FDA approved eighty-five drugs, only two of which can be traced in any meaningful way to academia. The hard truth is that industry builds drugs. If not for ALS's orphan status, there would be scores of companies developing compounds today, much as there are for Alzheimer's disease. Wyeth Pharmaceuticals alone has spent $450 million over the last five years on research and development for Alzheimer's drugs. In the same period, all U.S. pharmaceutical companies combined have spent precisely nothing on ALS.

Sharon and Sean dubbed their revolutionary plan the "ALS Manhattan Project."

"I liked the parallel," Sean said. The two were proposing "a way to gather a bunch of scientists and give them unlimited resources and access to technology in an attempt to solve a problem quickly." Sean and Sharon considered their plan the sensible way to declare war on ALS. But there was a hitch. "So there we were," Sean said, "with this plan to end all plans and no way to pay for it. We had a war with no soldiers, no tax base, no government to fund it."

JOHN MCCARTHY—former executive director of the International Health, Racquet & Sportsclub Association:

We were all surprised at how successful that first fund-raiser was. Six or seven people spoke at Augie's award ceremony, and they acknowledged to a man the importance of Augie to the success of everybody in the room. There are two people without whom the modern health industry wouldn't exist—Arthur Jones of Nautilus and Augie Nieto. Here was a chance for everybody in the business to pay back the debt we felt we owed one of the true fitness pioneers.

I like to think this effort will keep going, with or without Augie. Everybody in this business loves a party, particularly one with a purpose. I don't think anyone wants to see this party go away.

LYNNE:

I was uncomfortable with the idea of raising money until I spoke with my friend Linda. Her husband, Jack, was a very good friend of mine as well, and when he became ill, Jack asked me to throw a party for him after he was gone so Linda wouldn't have to think about it. I said I would, and we had a beautiful memorial service down on the beach and a wonderful party here in the house.

Before we started Augie's Quest, I told Linda I felt uneasy about the idea of raising money, of asking for help. Linda asked me how helping Jack had made me feel. I told her it was the only thing I could do, and I was grateful for the chance to do it. I'll never forget this. She said, "Let us have that."

Man of the Hour

———————◆———————

B Y LATE SUMMER of 2005, Augie's speech had
slowed slightly, but he was still perfectly intelligible,
and though the weakness in his arms and hands had advanced over the months since his diagnosis, particularly
in his right hand, his movement wasn't conspicuously
impaired.

He was still capable of strenuous exercise and managed most mornings to run five or six miles. This sort of
vigorous activity had always been his balm, and he was
persuaded his general fitness would help him stave off
the effects of his disease for as long as possible.

When Augie received the news that he would be

honored with a lifetime achievement award from his colleagues in the fitness industry, he wondered aloud among friends in the business if the event might serve as suitable occasion for an ALS fund-raiser.

The trade show where the award would be given traditionally ran for four days, from Thursday afternoon until midday Sunday. The weekend's events ordinarily included a slate of seminars, cocktail parties and banquet dinners, the occasional keynote address from an industry leading light, and long hours of examining elliptical trainers and treadmills, the latest in gym ventilation systems, locker room fixtures, free weights and weight stations, training togs, and vitamin supplements—the full range of supplies necessary for the successful operation of a modern gym. Augie couldn't be sure the trade association members would warm to the idea of transforming an award presentation into an ALS fund-raiser.

"Too often," Augie said, "these sorts of things feel like a shakedown," and he was reluctant to impose upon his colleagues in the industry.

A couple of Augie's friends, however, harbored no reluctance. Peter Brown, Augie's former sales manager, and Vinny Smith of Quest Software made overtures to the president of the International Health, Racquet & Sportsclub Association, John McCarthy, and to Wally Boyko, who effectively owned the show.

These men were responsible for organizing the event from year to year, and they both proved receptive to the suggestion of a fund-raiser. McCarthy and Boyko felt certain that Augie's friends in the fitness business would welcome the chance to contribute to Augie's cause and help Augie best meet his new challenge any way they could.

As longtime participants in the industry, McCarthy and Boyko were well aware that the gym business owed a substantial share of its robust financial health to Augie Nieto. Moreover, they were in a position to know that a preponderance of the association's members felt precisely the same way. By corporate standards, there are scores of American CEOs who have steered their companies to the pitch of success Augie enjoyed with Lifecycle Inc. and Life Fitness, but there are relatively few who have revolutionized their field. Armed primarily with vision and dogged persistence, Augie had breathed new life into the health club business at a time of industry-wide anemia.

By acting on his faith in cardio fitness, Augie had anticipated what would become a raging national trend and had helped to open health clubs around the country to an entirely new class of clientele—the non-weight-lifting cardio member—that today constitutes the bulk of U.S. gym business.

McCarthy and Boyko were convinced people across the industry, all of them acquainted by now with Augie's diagnosis, were anxious to give back to the man who had given them so much.

By this time, Augie was actively courting the Muscular Dystrophy Association as a partner for his fund-raising efforts. He was still some months away from a formal agreement with the organization and hoped a successful fund-raising event would provide him with the leverage he'd need to be a full participant in the MDA's ALS Division.

In the spring of 2005, while Augie was going through the dreary process of having his diagnosis reconfirmed, he'd met a local MDA representative at the offices of Dr. Robert Miller at Forbes Norris. This was not a chance encounter. Shannon Shryne, the MDA's director of business development in the San Diego office, had read of Augie's plight and knew of his corporate clout and his well-heeled circle of friends, and she had come to the MDA's clinic at California Pacific Medical Center expressly to introduce herself to Augie and see if they could work together to raise awareness of ALS, fund for its cure, or both.

Consequently, when talk surfaced of turning Augie's award presentation into an ALS event, Augie phoned Shannon to bring her into the discussion. When Shannon asked what the goals of the fund-raiser might be, Peter Brown told her Augie wanted to show his children he had made a significant contribution to his industry and had done good things in his life. Shannon also learned through Augie's friends that one of Augie's goals for the event was to be able to walk onto the stage.

By this time, Augie was deep in the literature of ALS and feared he would be confined to a wheelchair before September. "I had many people asking me how long Augie would live," Shannon said, "and if he'd be okay in September." These were questions put to Shannon as late as August 2005, when Augie was still jogging daily. "It just goes to show you how little people know about ALS," Shannon said.

Shannon and MDA district director Gretchen Bohrer set about soliciting sponsors and sending out invitations to Augie's colleagues and friends, and they were surprised by the enthusiastic response.

"When we made the calls, countless people were telling me how important Augie was to the fitness industry," she said, "and they really wanted to help." Fitness executives were quick to put their rivalries aside on Augie's behalf. Many agreed to buy banquet tables, which went for five, ten, and fifteen thousand dollars. By the end of August, Augie's initial ALS event already had the look of a rousing triumph.

Augie, however, was still nagged by misgivings. The September trade show was not a national gathering but a regional affair, and he couldn't be sure how well attended it might be. Furthermore, the weekend was already tied to the Ms. Fitness America pageant, and Augie feared the attendees might suffer from the effects of aesthetic whiplash, moving between the pageant and the banquet.

To judge by Shannon's experience, Augie's fears weren't altogether misplaced. "I found myself riding in an elevator with a seventy-five-year-old woman in a thong bikini," she recalled with a polite shudder. The weekend would be a blend of exposed abs and silent auctions, and Augie could only hope for the best.

Augie was to be presented the *National Fitness Trade Journal*'s Lifetime Achievement Award on the evening of Thursday, September 8, in the ballroom of the Rio Hotel. Silent auctions of donated exercise equipment would kick off the ceremony and would be followed by the award presentation before eight hundred of Augie's admiring colleagues. The honor of introducing Augie had gone to Charles "Chip" Baird, the founder of North Castle Partners in Greenwich, Connecticut.

Baird captured the essence of Augie's standing in the fitness industry when he noted that "walking with Augie through the trade show is like walking through an all-boys prep school with Angelina Jolie." Even a relative outsider to the business like Baird had no difficulty recognizing a comet in the fitness equipment industry when he saw one. "As an entrepreneur," Baird continued, "he is a legend, one of the few who achieve rock star status and the acknowledged celebrity of being known, like Cher, Madonna, and Sting, by only one name. You only have to say 'Augie.'"

The money came rolling in by the tens of thousands of dollars—from North Castle Partners, from Octane Fitness, Life Time Fitness, Fitness First Australia, 24 Hour Fitness, from Lynne Nieto's father, Jack Bransford, from various members of the Young Presidents' Organization, and from Ron Hemelgarn, the previous year's recipient of the award and an admirer of Augie's from the "emergency repair kit" days.

By the time the tally was in from the auctions and the

purchased tables and the straight donations, the event had raised $1,045,031, which distinguished it as the largest-grossing first-time event the Muscular Dystrophy Association had ever been associated with. By nonprofit standards, this was a rush job. The fund-raiser had been slapped together in just sixty days.

Augie had neglected to name his fund-raising organization as the event had approached, but just days before the function, Lynne dubbed it "Augie's Quest." The husband of one of Shannon's colleagues had drawn up the logo as a favor. Now, suddenly, Augie's Quest was promising to become a leading player in the field of ALS fundraising. And Augie himself, his rock star status confirmed in one industry, was about to test how well his clout might travel to another.

AUGIE:

In October of 2005, I was asked to give a speech the following August in Chicago. My biggest concern was whether my voice would be able to be heard. I had this big leap of faith for the first time, in that I was able to think more than ninety days out. I said yes.

I get incredible energy from the art of the speech. Most speakers don't take the time to personalize their message. I'll spend research time on each person who is going to be in the room. I know where they came from. I know what their parents do, and I incorporate them into my speech. People love to hear about themselves.

I brought my son, Austin. The audience was twenty-two- to twenty-six-year-olds. These were kids of Young Presidents' Organization members. I've been a member of the YPO since the mideighties. It's a worldwide association for CEOs under the age of fifty. There are probably eleven or twelve thousand members across the globe, and I imagine the YPO represents well over two trillion dollars in revenue worldwide. The organization itself and the friends I've made through the YPO have been incredibly significant in my life, so I was proud to be there, particularly with my son.

The program was devoted to life after graduation. The speakers were a Northwestern professor discussing the art of negotiation, a woman who specialized in dressing for success, and a member of the Hyatt family talking about what it was like to be in the family business. My goal was to give these kids a sense of what it's like to be vulnerable, since at their age they're fearless.

These kids were well-off and in need of direction, because they'd lived what I'll call a cocoonian life. Their parents had sheltered them from the hardships that had defined the older generation. That's something Lynne and I have wrestled with in raising our own children. How do you guide them so maybe money won't be the only metric of success. Maybe happiness. So I used my personal experience as a parent of our four kids. I had Austin in the front row.

I talked about my life as an entrepreneur. I talked about my business failures. I talked about the diagnosis. I talked about how the most important decision they would make in their life wasn't the career they would choose but the spouse they'd spend their life with.

You could have heard a pin drop. Fifty kids in the audience, all dead silent. There were tears that came from the girls first, and then everyone started crying, even the tough guys.

As I ended the speech, I used the quote "Life isn't measured by the number of breaths you take but by the number of times your breath is taken away." The kids were paralyzed. They couldn't move. They didn't know what to do.

They'd been struck by the randomness of life. You can prepare by going to all of the right schools, landing the right job, marrying the right person, and there are still factors you can't control. You can only control how you respond.

I don't believe they'd ever heard that from anyone. Mine was the dream career of every young adult. Everything about my life was envied, except for the diagnosis.

I knew then I had a new role in life. Whether I was dealing with adults or kids, I knew I had the ability to change their lives.

That night I was at the Navy Pier in a beer garden, and a young lady who'd been at the speech came up to me to talk about her father's cancer diagnosis. She wanted to know if I would help him transition into acceptance and not hide behind his work and his sense of duty to provide for the family. He was an old-school guy. He measured his worth by how much he provided.

I had three other people tell me similar stories. They felt they could share those with me because I had a unique perspective.

Austin came up to me toward the end of the night, and for the first time since the suicide attempt, he saw me again as a role model, and I once more saw the son I'd known.

I was like a wet noodle. I was emotionally spent, but Austin asked me to see one more person, a guy named Grant, and I said, "Okay, where is he?"

Grant came up to me and said, "You rocked my world." He then unbuttoned his shirt to show me his new tattoo. It went from one armpit to the other—two lines. He'd had the last thing I'd said tattooed across his chest: LIFE ISN'T MEASURED BY THE NUMBER OF BREATHES YOU TAKE BUT BY THE NUMBER OF TIMES YOUR BREATH IS TAKEN AWAY.

I looked at it, and I had three thoughts flash through me. Do I tell him he should be proud or that his parents are going to kill me or that I wish he'd used spell-check?

Life isn't measured by the number of breathes you take but by the number of times your breath is taken away.

His dad called me the next week. He was a CEO in the Detroit YPO chapter. He said, "This isn't how I would have chosen to have my son find the change he needed, but if this one tattoo will remind him of what it takes to be a good citizen, then that's something I'm indebted to you for."

Grant finally called me and said, "Why didn't you tell me about the typo? It hurt like hell to get it fixed."

Committee of One

———◆———

THOUGH JAMIE HEYWOOD, Sean Scott's associate
at the ALS Therapy Development Foundation in
Cambridge, had met Augie in the early summer of 2005,
the two hadn't hit it off. "Jamie told me that he thought
Augie didn't get him," said Sean. "I told him I'd give Augie
a call to see if I fared better. I'd heard about Augie's fund-
raising success from Sharon Hesterlee and figured we
could really use his help."

So Sean put in a call to Augie, and during their conversation Augie volunteered that he had a meeting scheduled at the Muscular Dystrophy Association's home office
in Tucson. Sean responded with news of his unofficial

collaboration with Sharon and provided Augie with a general overview of the research plan they'd been working on, the Manhattan Project for ALS. When Augie quizzed Sean about the state of the project, Sean offered up an education in the priorities and intricacies of the MDA's customary brand of medical funding.

The organization poured generous amounts of money into academic studies but was likely, according to Sean, to consider the ALS Therapy Development Foundation a bit of a "renegade organization." Sean couldn't imagine that his and Sharon's scheme to tackle ALS on a molecular level and start afresh with potential drug targets would win any champions at the MDA outside of Sharon's research group. Augie, however, found Sean immediately persuasive, and he shared with Sean his impatience with the traditional avenues of academic ALS research. Augie had seen quite enough of that manner of inquiry during his diagnosis tour.

Impulsively, Augie invited Sean to join his meeting with the MDA and insisted that Sean make a presentation as part of Augie's group—a group that would now include Augie and Lynne, Lynne's brother Kent, Sean, and slightly north of one million dollars from Augie's recent fund-raiser.

Sean met up with Augie at a Phoenix hotel and rode with Augie, Lynne, and Kent to Tucson in their rental car. Kent found himself in the backseat next to Sean and confessed to being mystified both by Sean's research plans and by Sean himself. Oncologists are ordinarily risk takers by nature. They're too often treating terminal cases and so are invariably pushing for more innovative therapies and are given to embracing the cutting edge, but here was a self-taught nondoctor, nonscientist advocating starting from scratch to seek a cure for ALS. That was a bit much, even for Kent.

Augie didn't share his brother-in-law's reservations. Augie and Sean hit it off immediately. Augie found Sean witty, informed, and refreshingly blunt about the state of medical research generally and ALS research specifically. Better still, from Augie's point of view, Sean's passion to find a cure for ALS was palpable, fiery even.

Sean was on a mission to vanquish the disease that had claimed his mother and could well claim him. He was not a research careerist and had no love for scientific life beyond his immediate desire to bring ALS to heel. Sean spoke eagerly of his plans to return to the world, once a cure had been found and the suffering had ended. Sean was not distractible. He shared with

Augie a driving passion to make all the Augies of the world well.

There was a considerable challenge, however, to the scope and prospective pace of Sean's Manhattan Project: expense. Sean was frank with Augie about what would be needed to fund research of the sort he envisioned. "I told Augie, 'You can't raise money fast enough for me. I'll break you. I'll outspend you at every turn.'" Sean acquainted Augie with the projected cost of his plan—sixty million dollars over three years.

"That's not the sort of number that's scary to a guy like Augie," Sean said. "I was talking about a comprehensive plan for destroying the disease, and though I clearly seemed unorthodox to him, my seven years of learning the landscape and my family history made him feel that our goals were aligned and that I had a handle on the problem." Before he'd met Sean, Augie had only developed a plan for raising money. Now he had one for spending it as well.

Word of Augie's fund-raising triumph had snared attention in the executive suite at MDA headquarters. In the realm of fund-raising, Augie was about as unorthodox as Sean. The MDA is best known for its annual Labor Day Telethon, hosted by Jerry Lewis, but also for its convenience store canisters and its boot drives in association with local firefighters. So the organization raises big money all at once for muscular dystrophy each September and collects smaller contributions steadily throughout the year.

Augie intended to put himself at the center of an ongoing ALS fund-raising effort and planned to brand himself as the face of ALS. So he wouldn't merely host fundraisers in the fashion of Jerry Lewis but would function as the cause and the bait. Then, once the money was raised, Augie meant to have full sway over how it was spent.

Augie was received in Tucson by Bob Ross, now deceased, who was the executive director of the association. Ross was celebrating his fiftieth year with the MDA, and most of his lieutenants had held their jobs nearly as long. The organization had been operating successfully and effectively for over half a century, and the corporate habits and practices of the MDA were pretty well entrenched. Augie showed up hoping to inspire a new urgency in the ALS division of the organization, and he began his meeting with Ross by telling him, "When I Google ALS, you show up on the second page."

Ross absorbed the charge without comment, but he shortly retired from the meeting and was heard quizzing his secretary in the outer office, "Do you know how to Google things?"

Ross and his executive colleagues, as successful as they'd been, were ripe to entertain overtures from the likes of Augie and were overdue for exposure to Augie's thinking on new approaches to ALS funding and, via Sean, ALS research. The organization wasn't hidebound exactly, but a dose of fresh insight couldn't hurt.

Augie had arrived close on the heels of his million-dollar fund-raiser, so he came armed with unalloyed credibility. Before the top MDA executives and a member of the MDA board, Dr. Stanley Appel, Augie proposed a new emphasis on ALS fund-raising and introduced Sean, who made a presentation on the ALS Therapy Development Foundation's latest mouse data and outlined its general approach to drug discovery. "I got a favorable response from the MDA staff," Sean recalled, "but no re-sounding endorsement." The fact, however, that MDA executives were even listening to a renegade like Sean Scott hinted at a general change in the atmosphere of the place.

Sean had become acquainted, through Sharon, with the appetite for more modern, aggressive practices that was prevalent throughout the lower levels of the MDA. Now Augie was bringing much the same attitude to the executive suite, where the men and women who ran the MDA had every reason to be satisfied with their accomplishments.

Much like the National Institutes of Health, the MDA's long-standing practice was to entertain grant applications from academic scientists and award funding to what it deemed were the worthiest projects. This was the traditional approach to medical research, and it produced methodical, exhaustive results that had, in more than a few instances, led to a more thorough understanding of disease and to effective drug therapies.

ALS, however, had long resisted this approach. Augie, from his layman's perspective, was tempted to compare the piecemeal grant process for ALS research to subcontractors designing the house they're building. The scientists identified areas of interest, developed pertinent theories, and applied for money to test those theories. That was a very different proposition from seeking to obliterate a disease by any means necessary. Sean said, "Augie came to the realization that 'Hey, nobody's in charge of curing me. Sean's not a lunatic. This is an actual problem.'" And it was an actual problem that Augie, with the MDA's help, was keen to address.

In the course of his meeting in Tucson, Augie floated

novel ideas about fund-raising and encouraged a new organizational emphasis on streamlined ALS research. He employed his considerable talents as a salesman to convince Ross and his colleagues—their historic success notwithstanding—that there still might be better ways to raise money and smarter ways to spend it.

Though it's little wonder Augie was persuasive—he'd been an exceptional salesman his entire adult life—it is to the everlasting credit of the MDA that its executives proved persuadable.

The MDA exhibited a willingness to veer and a capacity for entertaining new options. Augie was prepared to partner with the organization, but largely on his terms, and it was during this Tucson meeting that he presented Ross with a quintet of contract demands. Augie was intent that all of the money raised by Augie's Quest go exclusively to research. He insisted that he and Lynne maintain control over the research dollars. The funds raised by Augie were strictly to supplement the MDA's ALS budget. Augie's Quest was to pay only direct expenses and no overhead, and any donor relationship cultivated by Augie and brought to the MDA would help to fund Augie's Quest in perpetuity.

As contracts go, Augie's was a bit one-sided, but the

MDA's executives, to their credit, were content to let Augie have his way. The objections and points of debate all evaporated in fairly short order, and it was agreed that Augie's Quest would become part of the ALS division of the Muscular Dystrophy Association and would be chaired by Augie and Lynne. Augie's Quest would serve as an "aggressive, cure-driven initiative," and Augie made it clear in the meeting that he was after "accelerated results."

By meeting's end, Augie and his counterparts at the MDA had formed a transactional research advisory committee that would be tasked with finding worthy recipients for Augie's money.

The committee consisted of a half dozen academic clinicians and scientists and Sean Scott, inspired amateur. The first meeting was called shortly after Augie's visit to Tucson, and Sean found himself in a dispute almost immediately. The professors on the committee were, in Sean's opinion, overly sensitive to the process of doling out Augie's money. There was exhaustive talk of transparency in awarding the grants and the general academic ethics involved in who got how much and why.

Sean had no patience for this sort of thing. "I just wanted to contract out what needed to be done," he said, and he declared as much, to the dismay of his colleagues.

"They looked like they wanted to kill me and bury me in the backyard," Sean recalled.

When news of the dispute reached Orange County, Sean discovered he had an instinctive ally in Augie. As a patient himself, Augie had no use for quarrels about the ethics of distributing money to academia.

"He just about burst a blood vessel when he heard about the problem I was having," Sean recalled.

At the time, Sean's colleagues on the committee had been in the process of maneuvering him off the panel. Instead, Sean became a committee of one as far as Augie was concerned, and at that moment the focus of Augie's money and Augie's energy narrowed appreciably.

"When I look back at this time," Sean declared, "I realize Augie, as an entrepreneur, was acting in a fashion completely consistent with his investment principles. He came into a new landscape and spent a little time—first identifying the funding problem and second, the research problem. Then he started looking for solutions."

To Augie, that's exactly what Sean appeared to be—a solution. "In the end," Sean said, "Augie closed his eyes and bet on me like a horse."

AUGIE:

The academic research model is incredibly valuable to understanding the science of disease, but it's not set up to find a drug. We want to leverage the academic work, but there's a gap you'd think would be filled by big pharma. While big pharma will do development when it comes to a disease like ALS, they won't do research. They want to buy a proven pathway.

No one in the field of ALS is doing target discovery and then proving it in an animal. In other diseases—prostate cancer, breast cancer—there is ample research because the universe of patients is so large. All we're doing is applying big pharma technology to an orphan disease.

Part of the key to beating ALS is the business model. The perception by drug companies that ALS isn't a profitable disease is just wrong, and many of them don't know it yet.

Affymetrix Microarray
Scanners "R" Us

———◆———

THOUGH AUGIE WAS anxious to put the money he'd raised (and the money he intended to raise) to the most efficient and constructive use, he was faced immediately with the problem Sean Scott and Sharon Hesterlee had identified some months before. The lab at the ALS Therapy Development Foundation, under Sean's direction, had been swiftly and systematically running every pharmaceutical compound it could lay its hands on through its state-of-the-art SOD1 mouse model. TDF's scientists had also scrupulously retested every promising drug in the ALS literature, with particular attention to those compounds that had shown some efficacy in smaller-scale academic tests.

These retests, however, had failed to move the line. What had looked to be good effects in the initial academic tests had been washed out entirely in TDF's tests. Sean and his scientists failed to reproduce the reported results for any of the drugs they tested. No compound that had seemed to alter the progress of ALS in academic labs showed any effect at all once subjected to TDF's more rigorous protocol and more ambitious scale.

Practically speaking, nothing was working, and the accepted chemical pathways for treating ALS were fast becoming depleted.

Sean and his colleagues needed new targets, new pathways, so when Augie sought counsel from Sean and Sharon on the wisest aggressive use of the money he'd raised, they proposed a partnership aimed at discovering fresh targets for ALS drug development.

The Human Genome Project, sponsored jointly by the U.S. Department of Energy and the National Institutes of Health, had succeeded over the course of thirteen years in identifying and mapping the nearly thirty thousand genes in human DNA. The study had also identified 1.4 million locations where single-based DNA polymorphisms—or genetic variations—occur in humans. The project had spawned the development of revolutionary equipment, including microarray technology and supercomputers that allowed scientists to see more deeply into genetic processes and analyze information more quickly and thoroughly than ever before.

Sharon, Augie's principal consultant on the project, believed that microarray processing had matured sufficiently in the last few years to allow for speedy and, by medical research standards, economical genomic scanning, along with ambitious comparative analysis of DNA samples from people with ALS and people without it.

Here's where Augie's new relationship with the Muscular Dystrophy Association came in handy. The vast bulk of ALS sufferers in the nation almost invariably pass through one of the MDA's ALS clinics, which meant ample DNA samples were already on hand. The trick would be in persuading the clinics to part with them. Some clinicians gave voice to patient privacy concerns, while others held out for a financial stake in any therapy the survey might discover.

Augie solved the problem with his usual efficiency. The samples would be purchased for four hundred dollars apiece, which had the effect of clearing away all misgivings and caveats in a flash. The scientific work would be done by a nonprofit operation in Phoenix, the Translational Genomics Research Institute, better known as TGen. The study was projected to cost $1.3 million and would be conducted in the speedy, focused manner Augie insisted on.

Augie and Sharon visited TGen in October of 2005 and offered to put up half of the cost of the work if TGen would be responsible for the balance. Augie's Quest and TGen, Augie proposed, would also share equally in any financial benefits from the study in the form of licensed drug pathways. TGen was quick to agree to Augie's terms, and work on the project began in December of 2005.

The initial chore was to transfer the samples onto gene chips, which were in turn read by Affymetrix microarray scanners. The data was then analyzed by supercomputers capable of identifying any and all genetic variations between the ALS samples and the non-ALS samples.

This was no small task, given that each human cell contains nearly six billion DNA "letters," as they're called. DNA molecules are composed of four chemicals—adenine, cytosine, guanine, and thymine—which are customarily abbreviated as A, C, G, and T. The arrangement of these chemicals in a given DNA molecule renders it distinct from all other DNA molecules.

So the scope of the analysis would be monumental, but microarray technology has so evolved in the past few years that the time required for sifting through the genetic markers of an individual sample has dropped from weeks to days to hours.

The TGen team, consequently, was able to work through its entire inventory of gene chips in a few months, and it pinpointed variations in close to fifty genes that were common to people with ALS but rare in the general population. Through further analysis, TGen scientists succeeded in narrowing these genes of interest down to twenty-five that appeared to play a role in the disease.

Most significantly, the study found variations in genes with direct bearing on how nerve fibers interact with muscle fibers. Dietrich Stephan, TGen's director of neurogenomics and one of the lead investigators in the study, said the findings suggested that the genes in question "produce a sort of molecular glue that attaches motor neurons to muscles. It appears in ALS the nerve is able to peel off the muscle, and when that happens repeatedly, the nerve dies."

Ultimately, the TGen team identified fourteen targets of emphatic interest, and these targets are sufficiently varied in their genomic expression to suggest that ALS might arise from a stew of causes—genetic, viral, environmental—which spark the disease in combination.

From conception to the presentation of findings at a 2006 conference in Yokohama, Japan, the TGen study took a remarkably scant nine months to complete, years less than most studies of this magnitude take.

The TGen study serves as the epitome of Augie's approach to scientific discovery. These sorts of undertakings needn't be glacially slow, and though the results of the study were presented in a proper academic forum in Japan, Augie also advocated the release of the data on the Internet, where anyone might access it and review it. Additionally, the findings were accepted for publication in the prestigious *New England Journal of Medicine* and appeared in the August 2007 issue.

◆　◆　◆

WITH THE DISCOVERY of two dozen fresh chemical targets, Augie turned his attention to drug testing and development, Sean's specialty at the ALS Therapy Development

Foundation. Ever the entrepreneur, Augie had been study-ing the workings of the lab with an admiring but criti-cal eye.

When Sean's mother and Jamie's brother were diag-nosed with ALS, Sean and Jamie each embarked on a course of study that Augie was doomed to repeat six years later. They all soon discovered how pitifully little ALS therapy existed, and their examination of ALS-related clinical trials and grant-funded studies provoked in them a reaction against the academic model.

The original purpose of the ALS Therapy Development Foundation was to raise money to fund inventive and ag-gressive ALS research, the sorts of studies conducted by the manner of scientists who were thinking and working creatively on what was clearly, even to laymen like Sean and Jamie, a monumentally complicated disease.

It soon became apparent, however, that inventive and aggressive ALS research was in rather short supply. The ef-fort unearthed plenty of underfunded, plodding academic studies, but very little in the way of cutting-edge, stream-lined inquiry meant to lead to some sort of drug treatment as rapidly as possible. With close relatives as their primary customers, the duo couldn't afford the detachment of most scientists and professional fund-raisers.

Sean and Jamie were obliged to watch their loved ones' advancing symptoms and were determined to find, if not a cure, then a treatment adequate to slow the progression of the disease and so buy Sean's mother and Jamie's brother as much time as possible to wait for a breakthrough.

"There is nothing wrong with hypothesis driving science when you are down in the weeds and you are trying to test a very specific piece of cellular machinery," said Sean, "but when you are faced with a complete black box, when you have no idea what's wrong, there's no way to pick this problem apart one molecule at a time."

The lab's mandate would be to test all drugs that could conceivably have an effect on ALS. To that end, the foundation hired pharmacologists, veterinarians, chemists, and a score of technicians and began the work of establishing what would become the most extensive and ambitious mouse-testing laboratories in the world. Soon the foundation was paying the salaries of more than thirty employees, and TDF's financial obligations had climbed into the neighborhood of a half million dollars a month, which required unceasing and occasionally desperate fund-raising.

The shaky finances of the foundation were sure to make it difficult for Sean and Jamie to attract the sorts of biogenetic specialists they were bound to need to crack ALS. Nobody with a scrap of job security was likely to clamber on board TDF's slowly foundering ship.

As a highly motivated and interested observer, Augie had assessed the virtues and frailties of TDF. It was producing good science, but the revenue stream was uninspiring. "Sean and Jamie had unapologetically run their budget to redline every year," Augie said. "It wasn't irresponsible on their parts: it was a recognition that this was a rescue operation, not a career. They both felt that if you found the drug the day after your mother or brother died, that you'd still have lost. So they spent every dime they could grab as fast as they could grab it."

Jamie was the foundation's chief fund-raiser, and the expense of maintaining an operation as energetic and open-ended as TDF's mouse lab had upped the ante for the organization. Jamie simply couldn't stay far enough ahead of the swelling expenses to hope to stabilize TDF's financial footing.

Month after month, the organization came perilously close to exhausting its funds, so Jamie and his team were obliged to cultivate as many new donors as possible while frequently revisiting their old, largely tapped-out donors to request additional funding.

It was obvious to Augie that TDF would never survive as a predominately charity-supported institution. The lab showed considerable promise, and his exposure to Sean over the months since their initial meeting in Arizona had only served to buttress Augie's instinctive faith in the approach and rigor of TDF's drug-development testing.

As an ALS patient, Augie found the lab's devotion to turning over all rocks in its search for an ALS therapy deeply gratifying. As a businessman, however, he couldn't muster much enthusiasm for the financial drift of the foundation.

Augie had watched the workings of the ALS Therapy Development Foundation with enough attention to know that the organization would need to be tweaked considerably before his organization could make any sizeable investment. "I had great respect for their damn-the-torpedoes attitude," Augie said, but he also realized that the lab would require dramatically more investment and a stable financial architecture to survive. To that end, Augie struck a deal with Sean and Jamie and the controlling members of TDF's board.

Augie, in combination with the Muscular Dystrophy Association, would contribute eighteen million dollars to the foundation's drug-development program over three years, the largest single contribution in the storied history of the MDA. The money would complement the foundation's six-million-dollar annual budget. In addition to this grant, the MDA would continue to provide the lab access to ALS patients in its clinics across the country, which would mean ready availability of tissue and blood samples and a population eager to participate in drug trials.

In return, Augie would assume board chairmanship of what would now be called the ALS Therapy Development Institute, to better reflect the lab-driven nature of the endeavor. The promise of sustained funding and the full-throated endorsement of the MDA would put the institute on sufficiently solid footing to provide Augie, Sharon, and Sean with the credibility to lure a topflight scientist to head up the drug-discovery program. "Essentially," Sean said, "I was helping to hire a guy to take my job."

Together, the three narrowed the field of prospective candidates and began courting Steve Perrin of Biogen Idec, a scientist who'd collaborated with Sean for several years. The Therapy Development Institute's attack on ALS would produce enormous amounts of data, and Perrin was just the guy to make sense of it. "He ran a lab that did large-scale genomic profiling," Sharon remarked. "Steve is one of the experts who is really well versed in interpreting this kind of data. Chopping through it and pulling anything of value out of it is quite an undertaking."

When Perrin flew to Los Angeles to see Augie, he opened the meeting bluntly. "I want to be clear," Perrin said. "I care a great deal about ALS, but I think you've got a tough sell getting me into this project."

Undeterred, Augie put on a full-court press. "Augie was trying to get into Steve's head," Sharon recalled, "trying to figure out what made him tick. Augie was calling Steve at home, harassing him, really. He finally told Steve, 'Put your wife on the phone,' and Augie started talking her into the job." Augie would eventually seek to charm Perrin's mother-in-law as well. At length, Augie informed Perrin point-blank, "Be careful what you ask for, because you'll get it."

Ultimately, Perrin proved helpless against the onslaught. The physical move for Perrin was negligible. Biogen Idec and TDI are both Cambridge operations. But institutionally and philosophically, the change would be monumental. In accepting the job, Perrin was enlisting in a crusade and endorsing a radical approach to ALS research.

On the scientific side, TDI intended to take an entirely

fresh look at a disease first described a century and a half ago and break it down with every technology available, looking at every gene, protein, and virus in animal models and humans simultaneously. On the business side, the orphan status of ALS had its advantages that would likely allow the institute to garner more involvement from pharma and biotechnology companies. Under the terms of the 1983 Orphan Drug Act, any entity that develops a drug therapy for an orphan disease enjoys fast track FDA approval, seven years of market exclusivity, and no price caps on the drug developed.

In the end, Perrin took the job. "What could the guy do?" Augie asked. "We already had most of his original Biogen team hired on and waiting for him at the lab. We covered his salary, and his commute was a block shorter. Not only that, we needed him."

Augie:

My experience with charities in general is that they ask that you give them money and insist you trust how they're going to invest it. With Augie's Quest, I think we have a much more savvy donor or, as I call it, investor.

I've been to numerous galas where you believe you're doing the right thing. You've donated money. You think it's going into the hands of people who can help, but when you take a microscope to the process, you often end up finding that 80 percent of the money went to the band, the food, the experience, and hardly any of it went where you thought.

I don't want to feel like I'm a pity investment. I want people to trust me to spend their money well.

Brand ALS

—————◆—————

THE IDEA OF an annual fitness-industry fund-raising event for ALS had not actually occurred to Augie before a visit from Mark Mastrov, the founder of 24 Hour Fitness, an organization boasting almost four hundred health clubs in sixteen states and four countries, with an international membership of three million. Though Mastrov had been impressed with the money raised at the 2005 event, he took Augie to lunch so that he might inform him point-blank, "Great start. Now let's go raise some real money."

Mastrov's friend and business associate Lance Armstrong knew something about overcoming the odds when faced with disease, and Armstrong was quick to agree to participate in the 2006 Bash, as the event was called. Better still, he insisted on volunteering his time. Comedian and TV host Bob Saget, also a friend of Mastrov's, readily agreed to appear on the same terms.

The 2005 fund-raiser might have been slapped together by necessity, but the 2006 event was the product of extensive planning and preparation. In the summer preceding the Bash, Augie was still capable of driving, and Shannon Shryne recalled days when Augie would show up at her San Diego office bearing burritos for the staff as the prelude to an afternoon of hashing out the details of what was promising to be an extravagant evening.

The 2006 International Health, Racquet & Sportsclub Association convention was booked into the Las Vegas Hilton, which had a banquet room that could easily accommodate three thousand people. The previous year's event, piggybacked onto Augie's award ceremony, had been held at a much smaller venue and had been attended by a comparatively paltry eight hundred people. So the potential for donations would be far greater in 2006, but so would the potential for administrative headaches and general expense.

The Bash's organizing committee for 2006 decided

to mount the affair as an extravagant cocktail party, with elaborate ice sculptures, passed hors d'oeuvres, and multiple bars. Tickets were offered at a minimum price of three hundred dollars, and fund-raising professional Shannon professed shock at how fast the tickets sold. Augie's colleagues in the fitness industry snatched up all of the available sponsorships and VIP tables, and the event quickly sold out.

In a move typical of Augie's long-held business philosophy, he invited members of the Young Presidents' Organization to attend the Bash for free, no ticket required. Just as he had given away Lifecycles early in his career and had reaped extraordinary dividends, Augie calculated that a banquet hall salted with YPOers would make for livelier auctions and soaring donations, and once again Augie's instincts served him well.

The party was held on the evening of Wednesday, March 22, and the festivities commenced with a silent auction for items that included assorted pieces of top-of-the-line fitness equipment and a pair of boxing gloves signed by Robert De Niro. The admission take was $173,000, and the live auction that followed raised $175,000. Thirty-one thousand dollars of that came from the winning bid for one of Lance Armstrong's Trek bikes, and a forty-thousand-dollar bid took a game of one-on-one with Magic Johnson.

The Doobie Brothers provided the entertainment, and Armstrong spoke briefly and movingly off the cuff, acknowledging the surprisingly generous nature of the evening. "I think this event says a lot about Augie," Armstrong began, "the fact that everybody came together, regardless if they're from competing gyms or competing companies that make equipment. They all say, 'This is one of our own. This is a guy who has committed his life to our industry and who has been dealt a serious blow. We're going to be there for him. We're part of the quest.'"

The event raised nearly three million dollars in cash donations, and thanks to similar gifts of time and labor, the expenses of the Bash were kept remarkably low. In his comments, Armstrong had touched upon one of the exceptional features of the affair. Augie's colleagues had come together to support Augie and help fund his quest out of both corporate and personal gratitude.

It was commonly understood that Augie had shaped the fitness industry and was a key factor in the ongoing public appetite for health clubs and cardio exercise. But it was the personal flair and the good humor, the selfless compassion he'd exhibited in his life, that had left an indelible impression on his colleagues. They gave because they loved their careers and the man who'd helped provide them. The success of Augie's Bash was an unavoidable testament to the character of the man.

Additionally, Augie's colleagues could be assured that the money they were donating would be earmarked specifically for ALS research. There was no waste, no overhead, no extravagance in the Augie business model. This was Augie's new unconditional guarantee: give money to ALS research and have it spent on ALS research alone.

In this respect, Augie likes to say he anticipated the conditions Warren Buffett attached to his affiliation with the Bill and Melinda Gates Foundation. Buffett wouldn't stand for simply donating his wealth without also directing how the money would be spent. In the same manner, Augie gave his personal assurance—his figurative handshake—to each donor to Augie's Quest that their money would be spent wisely and well. Because he was Augie, and his colleagues knew him by history and reputation, they had no cause to doubt him.

On Labor Day weekend of 2006, Augie appeared alongside Jerry Lewis on nationwide TV. In his burgeoning role as the face of ALS, Augie presented a check representing total donations for ALS research raised since the previous autumn. Augie was still walking independently at the time, though his arms and hands were of little use to him and hung at his sides.

To make the presentation, Augie set his left arm swinging and had soon gained enough momentum to put a four-million-dollar check within the reach of Jerry Lewis, who plucked it from his hand.

That appearance marked a significant milestone in Augie's progression from failed suicide to ALS crusader. Augie Nieto had long been the handsome embodiment of the seductive virtues of exercise. He was the drive and philosophy behind Life Fitness. Now Augie had assumed a new challenge with a new goal. His disease was sufficiently rare and exotic to need not just an ambassador and a spokesman but a compelling victim, a Lou Gehrig for the modern age.

In leading the charge against his disease through fund-raising and the hands-on direction of a revolutionary approach to ALS research, Augie was making himself the planet's most conspicuous player in the realm of motor neuron disease. In both embracing his plight and warring against it, openly and actively, Augie Nieto was fast becoming brand ALS.

AUGIE:

If you have a brand—if you can create emotion and a feeling of pride—then nobody can take that away. Customers can rely on it.

When I first met with the MDA, I'd done my homework. I'd gathered a focus group of people, of donors, and I'd asked them what the MDA meant to them. They were all aware of the telethon, but not one person knew the MDA was the nation's largest funder of ALS research and had the most clinics around the country for ALS patients.

I knew I couldn't change the perception it had taken fifty years to generate, but I wanted to put a face on ALS and leverage all of the goodwill the MDA had earned through the years. So when we developed our Augie's Quest logo, I said I wanted "Augie's Quest" to be on the outer edge. I said I wanted to clearly describe the mission—"cure ALS." I said I wanted "MDA" in the middle because they're our core, our support.

Finally, I said I wanted a compass for the background so people would know that, even if we don't know where we are, we know where we're going.

Brother from Another Mother

———◆———

"I'M A BRAND GUY," Augie is fond of saying. It is a quality he cultivated as a child growing up in a house where most everything was inferior brand X. As the mastermind and CEO of Lifecycle and Life Fitness, Augie had done something uncommon in the industry. He had made himself the face of reliable gym equipment, had created a brand in a field where brands were largely meaningless. By attaching his personality and his story so very conspicuously to his products, Augie managed to make his Lifecycle brand both valuable and desirable. He was the fat kid who'd whipped himself into shape through rigorous exercise. He used the products he sold and served as proof of what they could do. The come-to-my-gym-and-look-like-me fitness club managers and owners of the era couldn't help but respond to Augie's story. His was a version of their own story writ large.

So Augie had won the sympathy of his customers through the appealing force of his personal narrative, and he cemented their loyalty to his products by making commerce personal as well. In a business where gym equipment was commonly abused, Augie personally guaranteed every Lifecycle, every treadmill, every rower, every elliptical trainer and weight station his company manufactured and sold. There were no caveats, no policy hurdles, no reams of punitive paperwork. If a machine broke, Augie replaced it. Period. And the guarantee was very much Augie's, his personal, ironclad assurance as the face of the company.

This sort of relationship between customer and supplier wasn't just new to the health club business, it was unique within it. Augie's firm belief in the value of brand names had been rewarded by his customers' ongoing loyalty to him. Now, in entirely different circumstances, Augie's faith in branding was about to be tested again.

Since his diagnosis, or more accurately, since his return from the brink and his acceptance of his diagnosis,

Augie had been sufficiently active in the world of ALS—
as a fund-raiser and a speaker and an acutely interested
patient—to have come to an understanding that the disease was an abstraction for most of the public. Of course,
that was partly due to the low incidence of ALS nationwide, but also to the mysterious nature of the disease and
its cruel, grinding way of robbing its victims of their personality and their humanity over time.

ALS is marked by a creeping ebb of individuality as
voluntary muscles throughout the body respond slug-
gishly and then not at all. It isn't uncommon for an ALS
patient, in the advanced stages of the disease, to see the
scope of his mobility reduced to a solitary finger or toe,
or perhaps just limited, labored eye movement. Commonly, ALS locks in its victims, and they're helpless to do
anything but think. This is the advanced state of ALS that
neurologist Stanley Appel refers to as "the human mind
in solo flight."

It had been a very long time since Lou Gehrig was
claimed by the disease, and no modern-day spokesper-
son had yet arrived on the scene. Near the end of 2006,
Augie began to entertain the notion of filling that vac-
uum as best he could. ALS needed a human face, a devoted advocate for a cure, and Augie had decided the job

was to be his, that his business career had more than prepared him to assume the responsibility.

Augie would be sick in the open for all to know and
see, which wasn't a decision he could make alone. If he
put himself in the public eye, Augie knew he'd be putting
his wife there as well, and given the degenerative nature
of ALS, Lynne was likely to assume the more prominent
role over time.

By mid 2006, Augie had lost much of the movement
in his arms and had to labor mightily to lift them. He had
trouble manipulating his fingers and needed help with
any activity requiring dexterity. He could still walk on his
own but, lacking the use of his arms for balance and with
growing weakness in his legs, he was a little unsure on
his feet.

By this time, speaking required considerable effort on
Augie's part, and even simple declarations were labori-
ous to deliver. So Lynne served as his aide and interpreter
when words failed him or emotion overtook him, either
at home among friends or on national television before
millions of strangers. Augie's determination to become
the face of his disease and bring ALS to the country's attention was no small matter, and Lynne signed on to the
effort with understandably mixed feelings.

Augie took the same go-big-or-go-home approach to publicity that he'd taken to research. On Labor Day weekend, 2006, Augie personally delivered a four-million-dollar check to Jerry Lewis during the MDA's prime-time telethon. That same weekend, Augie shared the cover of *Parade* magazine with thirteen-year-old Luke Christie, the MDA's 2006 national goodwill ambassador. Luke suffers from spinal muscular atrophy and is confined to a wheelchair. The article detailed Augie and Luke's conditions and told the story of how they met at an MDA board meeting in South Carolina.

"This little guy had the biggest heart in the room," Augie said. "His zest for life despite the hand he's been dealt is incredible. I've been a mentor, helping people build up their muscles. But living with a disease was a new experience for me, and I saw an opportunity to be mentored by Luke." These days Augie refers to Luke as his "brother from another mother," and the affection the two share is immediately evident in the article.

With his telethon appearance and the *Parade* article, which reached nearly eighty million Americans, Augie's story was seen and read in one weekend by the widest audience he could have possibly hoped for.

Naturally, the *Parade* article piqued interest in Augie

and his foundation. In October he contacted both the *New York Times* and the *Wall Street Journal* to offer exclusive access to whichever paper promised the best placement and broadest coverage of his story. The object was to bring attention not so much to Augie personally but to his bid to overhaul and accelerate the accepted practices of medical research.

The *Wall Street Journal* made the sweeter offer, and for several days in November Augie opened his life to a *Journal* reporter for what proved to be extensive page-one coverage under the headline "Trail of a Killer: A Fitness Mogul, Stricken by Illness, Hunts for Genes." While the piece provided cursory details of Augie's professional history, the bulk of the story was given over to the work of his foundation and to the state of medical research generally.

The *Journal* is, after all, a business-centric publication, so Augie's attempt to turn a Cambridge mouse lab into a highly efficient, for-profit ALS drug-therapy operation was a remarkably good fit for the paper. Augie was placed at the forefront of a trend in "privately funded gene quests" that take full advantage of technological advances, particularly supercomputers that allow for the rapid processing of DNA comparisons. The article coincided, to the day, with the official presentation of the TGen results at a conference in Yokohama, Japan.

Like the *Parade* article that had preceded it, the front-page *Wall Street Journal* story generated even more interest in Augie, both as an ALS patient and as a significant mover in the world of genetic research. Natalie Morales, a correspondent for NBC's *Today*, soon contacted Augie through the MDA to gauge his interest in appearing in a segment on his struggles with ALS and his dynamic approach to seeking a cure. The interview, conducted with Augie and Lynne at their home, was aired on December 28, 2006.

The Augie of the winter of 2006 had evolved appreciably from the grim, despairing Augie of the spring of 2005. Still walking capably at the time, he took a stroll with Morales on the beach overlooked by his house and expressed to her a sentiment that would never have occurred to him on that dark Memorial Day weekend a year earlier. "Instead of mourning what I can't do," Augie said, "I choose to celebrate what I can do."

Augie's cheerful presence and optimistic attitude struck a decisive chord with viewers, especially those who had a family member or friend with the disease. Augie's foundation was immediately swamped with correspondence.

"I want to thank you for all you've done," a typical e-mail read, "to help bring a light to this little known illness." Another viewer remarked, "Your attitude is an inspiration to us all."

Augie heard directly from a number of ALS sufferers who voiced their frustrations with the ravages of the disease as well as with the slow progress in developing effective treatments. Augie's crusade served as a candle in the darkness. "Thanks to the huge breakthrough announced by TGen," one Arizona patient wrote, "me, my family, and the entire ALS community now have a level of hope like never before."

Halfway across the country, in Vicksburg, Mississippi, a sixth-grade public school English class fell under Augie's spell. The teacher, Mille G. Wolfe, had lost a childhood friend to ALS in 2004, and she and her students had studied the disease and its victims. They read *Tuesdays with Morrie* and came across news of Augie and his organization in *Parade* and on *Today*. Moved by Augie's plight and his good-humored grace, the students decided to raise money for Augie's Quest.

Vicksburg has not been affluent since cotton was king. Best known as the site of a bloody siege during the Civil War, the city recovered from the hostilities and thrived as a river town until the demise of paddle wheel steamboats. Eventually, even the great Mississippi abandoned the place when it shifted west, leaving Vicksburg on a tree-choked backwater. Revitalization has taken anemic hold on a block or two of the downtown. Otherwise, the town is dusty and decaying, with only hints of its past grandeur.

Though a bit threadbare on the outside, Bowmar Avenue Elementary School is spotless within and is public in the best sense of the word. The student body is a jumbled blend of black, white, and Hispanic, and the kids are conspicuously alive to knowledge and unfailingly polite in the courtly fashion common to the Deep South. Mille Wolfe's students weren't content merely to write essays about what they'd learned of ALS. Augie had inspired them to do more.

The class organized a craft sale. They made items that would be offered for purchase to the community at large—needlework, paintings, and bits of homespun marquetry. They then sold coupons with which the items could be bought. The event raised a startling $4,600.

All correspondence to Augie's Quest passes through the MDA's San Diego office and is read by Shannon Shryne or her assistant. On a sunny March afternoon in

2007, Shannon showed up at Augie's house with a bundle of mail—chiefly birthday cards for him—and a lone, hand-lettered envelope, separate from the rest. "You're not going to believe this," Shannon told him.

Shannon extracted the letter written by Ms. Wolfe on behalf of her class and read it to Augie. Ms. Wolfe described how the class had happened onto Augie's story, what they'd learned of his disease, and how they'd been moved to respond. "Please accept our contribution," Ms. Wolfe wrote, "and know that a small group of gifted Mississippi students is pulling for you and praying for a cure."

Shannon then showed Augie the check that had been tucked in a fold of the letter. Somewhat mysteriously, certainly unexpectedly, Augie had reached the students of an English class in a public school in faraway Mississippi and had inspired them to care more deeply about him and his disease than they and Augie together might have anticipated. The letter came as a pleasant surprise; the check as an outright shock.

Augie responded like most any of us would. Augie wept.

AUGIE:

I have a machine I nicknamed Thumper. It pounds my chest and breaks up the mucus. I have a cough assist that throws air down my throat and then sucks out the mucus. I have a BiPAP ventilator. I have a feeding tube. I have a diaphragm pacing system.

When I was diagnosed, there was only one drug for ALS—Rilutek. It costs twelve hundred dollars a month and extends your life for maybe ninety days. I take a drug to level out my emotions. I take an antioxidant. I take lipoic acid, but I don't remember why. I take fish oil for my heart. I took tamoxifen for a while, a female hormone. My doctor asked me, "How's your libido? You probably can't perform."

I was doing fine before he brought it up.

PATRICK FUSCOE—Augie and Lynne's friend and fellow YPO member:

Last spring Augie and Lynne invited me and my wife, Bonnie, to join them on their boat for a short weekend trip. Augie was well into the effects of ALS.

On Saturday morning, Augie insisted on a swim. That seemed impossible. With no arm movement and very little leg mobility, we couldn't conceive of how Augie might manage it. Nonetheless, he devised a plan that called for a large water ski jacket and scuba fins.

We suited him up and lowered him into the ocean using the dinghy davit, three pairs of arms, and the encouragement of his trio of barking dogs. Augie loved the propulsion he could muster with the fins as he bobbed upright like a cork.

I swam alongside, and we coaxed the Labrador pup, Hazel, to leap repeatedly from the stern swim step. She'd flail in a panicked rush through the water right up and over Augie's head. Augie couldn't stop laughing.

Augie and I kicked our way near the beach, and Augie decided he wanted to go up onto the shore. The beach was steep and rocky, but we managed to climb out after a while and labored across the stones.

It took us nearly half an hour to go about ten yards across the rocks and over a small wall toward a boccie ball court. Augie had a tactful, respectful way of directing my help. He mixed encouragement with some humor, usually at his own expense.

The place was abandoned, and Augie challenged me to a game of boccie for a beer. Though he was handicapped by a lack *of balance and dangling arms, Augie would rock his throwing arm with his shoulders and then release the ball at just the right moment. I was trying like hell to beat him, and I still lost.*

Lynne:

ALS causes spasticity in your bladder, and Augie had had a couple of incidents where he'd waited too long and couldn't get to the bathroom. There's a medication for that, and his doctor told us it worked and there were no side effects, but Augie said, "I don't need it," and he wouldn't take it.

We'd been out to dinner one night with our friend, and Augie's former colleague, Peter Brown, and I was parking the car. Augie and Peter were walking down the driveway, steps from the house, when Augie said, "I've got to go. I've got to go right now."

So Peter pulls Augie's pants down, and I walk up to find Augie peeing not just on the driveway but all over the front of his pants. Augie and Peter were laughing about it, but I was mad, and I walked over and smacked Augie. I meant to hit him in the stomach, but I guess I swung a little lower than that.

Augie crumpled up and went straight down onto his ass. He

was fine, and we all had a good laugh. He started taking the blad-der pill the next day.

I decided, from there on out, if I wanted my way with Augie, I'd just punch him in the nuts.

Out of the Shadows

———◆———

GIVEN HIS PERSONAL resources, Augie can afford equipment and treatment that might be out of reach for most ALS patients. In fact, thanks to his self-sought high profile in the ALS community, he considers it his obligation to try any and all therapies his doctors and consultants approve of and then present himself as a guinea pig for measuring the results. No easy thing with ALS. The standard response among patients, when pronouncing on the efficacy of ALS drug therapies, runs something like this: "I don't know if it's working because I can't say how much worse I'd be if I weren't taking it."

Neurologists in the field are frequently given to a similar

view, which makes it difficult for patients to dispense with treatments once they've embarked upon them. Furthermore, the I-can't-stop-taking-it-now approach makes it especially important that ALS drug therapy have a low level of toxicity, since the course of treatment is likely to be open-ended.

Augie's approach to ALS therapies is much like his approach to business generally. "I look for treatments," he says, "that offer minimum risk with a maximal upside." By this point, Augie knows too much about ALS and has too much access to leading experts in the field to find temptation in chasing after the current crop of miracle cures for the disease. Due to the devastating nature of ALS, there is a growing catalog of pseudotreatments and a patient base—known in the community as PALS, or *people with ALS*—that is understandably desperate for almost any therapy on offer.

Currently, a Chinese neurosurgeon, Dr. Hongyun Huang, is drawing patients to his Beijing clinic with a twenty-thousand-dollar procedure that calls for the injection of fetal tissue (more precisely, olfactory ensheathing cells) into the forebrain and spinal cord of ALS patients. There is, at this point, no definitive evidence that the treatment is effective in producing any sort of measurable return in mobility, but some patients who've received the injections have made anecdotal claims of general improvement.

Neurologists are less charitable in their assessment of theratic therapy, offered in Mexico. The treatment is based on the theory that both ALS and MS are caused by viruses, a distinct possibility but hardly an established fact. At a Monterrey clinic, patients undergo two hours of exposure to a "Bio-Oscillating Frequency Ring," followed by massage and hydrotherapy.

In a similar vein, a Stateside clinic promotes scalar wave technology, which promises to disengage clumped red blood cells and promote muscle health. As of yet, there is no sound medical basis for either therapy.

Antimycoplasmal treatments are driven by the suspicion that ALS is caused by chronic infection. The theory has been fueled, in large part, by a Department of Defense study on the high incidence of ALS among veterans of the Gulf War. Mycoplasmal infections often attend the disease in these cases.

There is reason to believe that exposure to heavy metals plays a role in the development of some cases of ALS, possibly on the Japanese peninsula of Kii, for instance. Chelation therapy, or dental amalgam removal, addresses the threat by replacing gold and metal fillings with porcelain.

Finally, there are no end of nutritional and holistic approaches that claim to treat ALS with herbs and vitamins and "glyconutrient" agents. Augie sought treatment from a Tibetan healer in San Diego for about six months. He was administered nutritional supplements that, according to Lynne, "looked strangely like rabbit droppings." Augie neglected to follow the healer's strict nutritional recommendations, and he flatly refused to give up wine. There was no measurable change in the course of the disease.

Therapies such as this one tend to fall into the category of, at worst, harmless and, at best, marginally effective. What emerges from the welter of treatments offered worldwide for ALS is a distinct sense of how intricately complicated and veritably confounding the disease is and how desperate the appetite for a treatment.

Since ALS presents differently in different patients, progresses variously and at varying rates, and appears to arise from a range of causes, which might include locale, genetic disposition, viral exposure, and other unknown triggers, the temptation among PALS to chase an experimental treatment or an exotic offshore wonder drug is perfectly understandable. A pharmaceutical dustup is going on now that captures in its thorny essence the seductive pull of new ALS drug therapies and the maddening frustrations of waiting for FDA-sanctioned compounds to work their way through the rigorous approval process.

The drug in question is called Iplex. It is composed of a growth hormone known as IGF-1 (insulin-like growth factor 1) that has been blended with a binding protein that permits the hormone to linger in the blood.

The rationale for trying the drug on ALS patients is that the growth factor might prolong the life of otherwise dying motor neurons and so help sustain and bulk up affected muscles for as long as possible. Another form of IGF-1 called Myotrophin was developed by Cephalon, an American biopharmaceutical company, and tested on ALS patients in the United States and Europe several years ago.

The U.S. results qualified as positive. The drug appeared to account for a modest improvement in life span. In the European test, however, Myotrophin was much less effective and seemed, in some cases, to be harmful. A third, tie-breaking test is presently under way in the United States. Still considered experimental, Myotrophin hasn't been approved by the FDA and isn't available in the United States.

Insmed, the producer of Iplex, which is a combination of IGF-1 and IGF binding protein 3, recently lost a patent dispute with yet another U.S. pharmaceutical company that makes an IGF-1 compound for treating short stature. The two companies struck a deal that allows Insmed to test Iplex in the United States exclusively for the treatment of myotonic dystrophy, the most common from of adult-onset muscular dystrophy.

The Italian Ministry of Health entered into a deal that allows Insmed to export Iplex to Italy on a compassionate basis. The drug is currently being tested in Italy on ALS patients. To further complicate matters, Cephalon owns the patent on IGF-1 to treat ALS, so it's unclear what would become of Iplex if it proved effective against ALS in the Italian trial. Or rather, it is painfully clear what would become of Iplex: it would be the subject of lengthy litigation.

The lumbering and litigious nature of the development and testing of these various formulations of IGF-1 is precisely what infuriates ALS patients and their loved ones. As motions are filed and the patent office deliberates, motor neurons die, muscles atrophy, function ebbs. The disease pursues its dogged course. So it's not surprising that

ALS sufferers turn to alternative treatments, damn the expense, and have embraced Augie's assertive and increasingly public bid to streamline medical research and drug development in his quest for safe, effective treatments for ALS.

Augie's well-publicized approach to the business of drug discovery, organized along the successful lines of his previous career, and his unflinching determination in the face of the bottomless challenges ALS supplies have made him a stellar presence in the PALS community. The business of research has traditionally been segregated from the patients the research is intended to serve, but Augie combines the two by being both TDI chairman and ALS sufferer. Augie's reputation as a businessman and his inherent status as a person with ALS have helped attract his fellow patients to join him. Many of them were casting around for some organized approach to treatment and were looking for a way to help support the search for a cure through fund-raising and personal donations. In Augie's Quest they have found an organizer and an organization dedicated to both.

Augie has helped draw ALS sufferers into the light. His own experience made him aware of how devastating the diagnosis can be and how very tempting denial and reclusive retirement can seem to someone grappling with the disease. By showing himself and his symptoms openly, by treating a cure for ALS like a manageable business proposition, and by trafficking conspicuously in hope, Augie has engineered a new paradigm for ALS and has drawn a full complement of patients to his side.

One of them is Phil Carlo, a fifty-seven-year-old writer based in New York, who was diagnosed with ALS in 2004. In his search for drug therapies and cutting-edge ALS treatments, Carlo had come across news of a surgeon in Cleveland, Dr. Raymond Onders. Assisted by a team of biomedical engineers at Case Western Reserve University, Onders had developed what he called a "diaphragm pacing system" (DPS). The object was to help people with compromised diaphragms breathe without the aid of a conventional ventilator. His approach called for the placement of a pair of electrodes and a solitary ground in the diaphragm wall via laparoscopic surgery. The leads were then connected to an external battery pack that emitted measured electrical impulses, causing the diaphragm to contract. As a result, air would be drawn into the lungs.

The DPS "conditions" the diaphragm and strengthens the muscles to the point where a previously ventilated patient can be ventilator free. By mid-January 2007, Dr. Onders had performed the procedure on forty-six patients, thirteen of them with ALS. The preponderance were victims of spinal cord injury, including Christopher Reeve, who was the third patient to receive a diaphragm pacing system. Eventually, Reeve was able to go off his ventilator for a few hours a day.

Carlo saw enough promise in the procedure to contact Dr. Onders, and in March of 2007, Carlo flew to Cleveland for the surgery. At his home on the West Coast, Augie was also keeping current with the latest in ALS treatments, and he too had heard of Dr. Onders's diaphragm pacing system. When Augie called Dr. Onders to make inquiries, he was given contact information for patients who'd already received the surgery, and one of those patients was Phil Carlo. Augie dialed him up to ask about his experience with the DPS, and Carlo, in turn, took occasion to quiz Augie on some of the details of the *Wall Street Journal* coverage.

Carlo found Augie to be an inspiring specimen, an ALS patient grappling publicly with his disease and leveraging everything he'd learned in a triumphant business career to try to overhaul medical research for the express good of his fellow patients. By the time he spoke to

Augie, Carlo was psychologically ready to make the acquaintance. "I hadn't wanted to go public with this disease," Carlo said. "I just felt it was nobody's business, but then I came to realize it might be good if I could give voice to the genuine reality of what it's about. To talk about the problems with finding a cure."

Carlo, like countless other ALS patients, took inspiration from Augie's frontal assault on the conventional approach to the disease they all share. "What Augie is doing," Carlo said, "is what needs to be done." Thanks in large part to Augie, Carlo is now out in the open with ALS and is determined to do everything he can "to let the world know about this miserable disease."

The hope and optimism that mark Augie's Quest and that cling to the man himself have proven to be contagious within the ALS community. Phil Carlo, in fact, is just one of many ALS patients who have been energized by Augie's enthusiasm for the work he has undertaken. Augie's insistence on engineering a cure for ALS with all deliberate speed and the hope he exudes that the disease can and will be vanquished in the near term have served to galvanize his fellow patients.

ALS has long resisted not just a cure but also a cogent sense of what brings on the disease and how its advance might best be blunted. Theories abound, but there exists, as yet, no effective defense against ALS, hard news to digest for an ALS patient fresh from his diagnosis. The natural temptation is to retreat into the embrace of family and hope for a miracle. Augie could well have done that himself. As a man of considerable means, he could easily have gathered up his wife and children and traveled the world for as long as he was able, keeping current with developments in ALS therapy but not actively inciting any.

Sean Scott has personally known more than one hundred ALS patients, including his own mother, and he marvels at Augie's drive and energy in the face of the disease's relentlessly punishing effects. "Jamie Heywood and I were shouldering the burden for our relatives," Sean said when describing his clinical involvement in ALS. "Augie is doing this himself. It's remarkable."

Augie:

The mother of a friend of ours lives down in Laguna, where Mitch Albom has a home. After hearing about our diagnosis, she was out walking her dog one day and saw Mitch in his yard. She stopped to talk to him and told him about me. She said she'd bought a copy of Tuesdays with Morrie she wanted him to sign for me.

Mitch said he'd do her one better, and not only did he sign it, but he brought it to me one afternoon. Mitch came with his wife. I'll never forget it. He walked right in, pulled up a chair, and sat down right in front of me like nobody else was there. We talked for a long while, just me and him. About ALS. About Morrie. About hope and strength and grace. It was a fine afternoon.

Lynne:

They were very nice people. Just after our diagnosis, we'd been given two copies of Tuesdays with Morrie, which was two too many at the time. But we were ready for it by the time we met Mitch.

It was kind of them to come. Unfortunately, we've got this tricky driveway, and when we were outside seeing them off, they backed into the wall. And with an audience. No good deed, huh?

AUGIE:

Just before he left, Mitch asked me if there was anything he could do for me, anything at all. That's exactly the wrong question to ask me. I told him about our fund-raisers, particularly about the one coming up, and I told him it would be great if he could serve as the keynote speaker for the 2007 Bash in San Francisco.

Mitch said he'd be on book tour in Australia at that time, but he'd find a way to get there. And he did. That's the amazing thing. He gave a great speech and refused to accept any payment. He made an enormous effort to be there. It really meant a lot to us.

What Kind of World
Do You Want?

————◆————

IN ADDITION TO spearheading a revolution in disease
science, Augie is also inviting those in the PALS community to take ownership of what happens to them and
why. Augie has given not just hope to his fellow patients,
but has inspired them to hold public fund-raising events
and channel much-needed cash into the sort of efficient
and forward-leaning research that Augie is convinced
holds the greatest promise for a cure.

To that end, Augie had already presided over a pair
of remarkably successful fund-raising events, what had
come to be known as Bashes, for Augie's Quest. The 2007
version was scheduled for March 30 in San Francisco

during the International Health, Racquet & Sportsclub Association's twenty-sixth annual convention.

The event would occupy the Marriott Hotel's forty-thousand-square-foot Yerba Buena Ballroom on Saturday night. Unlike the previous Bash, this year's event would be a banquet for one thousand rather than a cocktail party for three times that many, and the event would focus specifically on ALS. True to its name, the 2007 Bash would be a party, but a party with a pronounced theme and a suitable guest speaker in the person of Mitch Albom.

It's fair to say that Albom's *Tuesdays with Morrie*, his book about his former professor's battle with ALS, thrust the disease into the public consciousness. With eight million copies sold and an Oprah Winfrey–produced TV version of the story, *Tuesdays with Morrie* was virtually unavoidable. Albom has subsequently published a pair of best-selling novels, but he remains a compelling ambassador for the wit and insight of his former professor and an eloquent witness to the devastating progress of Morrie Schwartz's disease.

If Lance Armstrong, the previous year's keynote speaker, addressed triumph over adversity generally, Albom would speak to ALS specifically and thereby focus the event on the considerable task at hand—finding a cure.

The hostess of the evening would be multiple Olympic medalist Summer Sanders, with singer-songwriter John Ondrasik as the musical headliner. Ondrasik, ordinarily accompanied by the members of Five for Fighting, would be playing a solo set. Augie had sought out the singer due in significant part to his daughter Lindsay's fondness for "100 Years," Ondrasik's number-one hit single from 2004's *The Battle for Everything*. Ondrasik had responded to Augie's invitation with unanticipated enthusiasm. It turned out Ondrasik had a friend with ALS, along with a pronounced compassionate streak.

The event began Friday evening in the concourse outside of the ballroom with cocktails and numerous silent auction items on display for bidding. Shannon Shryne in particular had labored to assemble an irresistible roster of goods for auction. Among them were pieces of autographed sports memorabilia; cases of scarce wine; a ride with Stephen Hawking on a zero gravity "vomit comet"; and weeklong stays at a villa in Hawaii, on a yacht in the Virgin Islands, and at a resort in Australia.

Augie and his team had early reason for optimism. Sponsorships for the 2007 Bash had been offered at anywhere from three thousand to fifty thousand dollars and included admission to the banquet and a table for ten toward the front of the hall. The generosity on display from the sponsors was already well ahead of the standard established in 2006. "The people who gave fifteen thousand dollars were giving fifty thousand dollars," Augie said. "It's almost like we proved to the industry last year that we could all come together." The room had long since sold out at close to one thousand guests.

With ALS research minutes costing nearly seventy dollars apiece, the price of one day's clinical research runs to thirty-two thousand dollars, which means that a one-million-dollar donation will be burned through in about a month. The price tag of running to ground a complicated neurogenetic disease like ALS is likely to be dauntingly enormous, so it was Augie's ongoing task to keep the fund-raising ball rolling. Fortunately for him, many of his colleagues had kicked off their own fundraising efforts to help sustain the flow of research dollars between Bashes.

Augie's old friend Ron Hemelgarn had independently mounted a fund-raising effort in his Toledo, Ohio, fitness club. "We had these round mobiles with Augie's picture on one side," Hemelgarn said, "and pictures of other

people with ALS on the other side." The mobiles were offered for sale to club members at whatever price they
would pay.

"The trainers would tell the members about Augie's
Quest and how Augie was behind the Life Fitness products," said Hemelgarn. "We had some people give a dollar;
some gave ten dollars; some gave one hundred dollars."
The purchased mobiles were then affixed to walls in the reception area of the gym, with the name of the donor written on each. The project raised $4,600 for ALS research.

At gatherings like the IHRSA trade show, Hemelgarn
is a tireless advocate of this sort of fund-raising among
his colleagues on the gym-ownership side of the business. Hemelgarn has done the math and recognizes the
potential clout of twenty-nine thousand health clubs nationwide. "We're talking major money," he enthused. If
each club in the nation replicated Hemelgarn's effort in
Toledo, the industry would produce a whopping $130
million in ALS research funds. As this style of home-
grown fund-raising increasingly takes hold throughout
the fitness business, Augie's annual Bash promises to become the icing on a rather sizeable cake.

For now, though, the Bash remains the industry-wide
focus of attention for Augie's cause, and the 2007 install-

ment would only serve to reaffirm the high feeling for Augie that permeates the fitness industry. Bids on the silent auction items were closed out as the banquet hall doors opened to reveal a generic hotel space transformed into an elegant dining room for one thousand, with a high-tech stage at the head of the hall. The stage was equipped with massive, ballpark-quality Diamond Vision screens to bring every detail of the proceedings to the back of the house.

The crowd was shown a video presentation of the previous twelve months' accomplishments in ALS-related research, including the results of the TGen project that had led to the identification of twenty-five specific genes implicated in the development of ALS. That news served as prelude to the introduction of Albom, who described the gentle wit and crooked smile of his former anthropology professor.

Shannon Shryne, in remarking on the 2006 Bash in Las Vegas, had described it as an extravagant cocktail party, replete with ice sculptures and exotic hors d'oeuvres. While raucous and highly successful, the 2006 Bash hadn't focused on the specifics of ALS from the perspective of patients or researchers. The 2007 Bash had been organized to keep the spotlight squarely on the disease, and Albom's talk was a key element in the evening's theme.

On the topic of ALS and its effects upon his friend and professor, Albom was funny and illuminating and gave the audience a clear layman's account of the highly complex neurological disorder. In just twenty minutes, Albom had brought a debilitated Morrie Schwartz fully to life only to see him into his grave, so the crowd was already primed for tears when Albom concluded by introducing Augie and Lynne, who joined him on the stage.

For many at the event, this was the first time they'd seen Augie in a wheelchair. His balance had become unreliable by the end of 2006, but he had avoided any real trouble and had successfully calmed Lynne's fears. On a January trip to Las Vegas, however, Augie stumbled coming out of a hotel elevator. His arms were fully immobile by this time and couldn't help him break his fall. He pitched directly onto his face and came away with chipped teeth and blackened eyes. That episode served as proof enough for both Augie and Lynne that the time for a chair had come.

In keeping with Augie's nature, his would be no ordinary wheelchair. Augie did his homework on the technology available in power chairs and decided on what is grandly called the Ibot Mobility System. The chair—and it is more a chair than a system—is cousin to the Segway scooter and shares an inventor in Dean Kamen. Like the scooter of Kamen's design, the Ibot chair maintains balance electronically through a combination of sensors, software, and gyroscopes.

The tandem wheels on either side of the chair are capable of pivoting to carry the user up and down staircases. Better still, the wheels can go on end and elevate the user to eye level. The sensors and gyroscopes in combination allow the chair to balance on two wheels, ever finding the user's center of gravity with a gentle rocking motion.

So, following Albom's introduction, Augie did take the stage of the 2007 Bash in a wheelchair, but *what* a chair. A few of Augie's engineering friends had been eyeing the contraption earlier, and the chair had been the source of animated conversation.

But the sight of fitness-industry icon Augie Nieto reduced to rolling across the stage rather than striding across it surely brought home to the crowd the degenerative destructiveness of ALS. The symptoms of the disease are, generally speaking, slow to materialize and aren't especially dynamic. Since ALS is marked by a loss of motor function, its progress is measured in deficits. The motion an ALS patient has mastered to bring a fork to his mouth may work successfully one month but not the next. The ability to dress, to walk, to speak—all can ebb gradually and gently over time or erode more rapidly and then simply vanish as the affected motor neurons cease to function.

Either way, the end result is a negative circumstance, the absence of animation as the disease deprives its victim of the ability to move, to speak, and finally to breathe. The Augie before the crowd at the 2007 Bash was greatly reduced from the Augie many of these same people had seen the year before. His drive and determination were, if anything, stronger, but his body had clearly betrayed him through the months.

With Augie on the stage in his motorized chair, ALS was no longer an abstraction for anyone present. Its power to grind down and destroy even the healthiest specimen was on full display. Rather than calling for donations for a cure, the sight of Augie before his friends and colleagues served as a stark demand for them.

Augie, with Lynne at his side, made a brief, emotional address to the crowd. The pair then yielded the stage to Ondrasik, who accompanied himself on both the piano and the acoustic guitar. He played for forty-five minutes, mixing hits like "Superman" with newer and more obscure songs. The set was building toward an emotional climax planned for Augie by his friends at the Muscular Dystrophy Association but kept secret from Augie and Lynne.

Ondrasik's final number would find him at the piano for his hit song "100 Years." The opening notes cued a video presentation of scores of photographs of Augie from childhood onward. During the late-afternoon sound check, Ondrasik had been obliged to close his eyes while he played. "I can't watch," he'd said. "It's just too hard."

The photos of Augie—as a boy, as a young man, as a vibrant executive, as a doting husband and father—combined with Ondrasik's ode to life and love, had an almost debilitating effect. The video and the song, experienced together, approached emotional cruelty.

During the afternoon's rehearsal, Ondrasik had been reminded of a similarly charged performance he'd given, this one in the wake of 9/11. "I was playing 'Superman' at the concert for New York," he'd recalled, "and I could see these big firemen, burly guys, just sobbing. I couldn't watch then either." On a more personal level, the images of Augie's march through the years had had much the same effect on Ondrasik. He'd been able to play well enough and sing while the photos emerged and then dissolved on the screen, but he hadn't been able to watch.

"There are few people who focus you on your life and make you look at it through a correct prism," Ondrasik had said once he'd finished the ordeal of the sound check. "My daughter is one. Augie is another."

By song's end, the entire hall was near emotional collapse, but John Ondrasik wasn't quite finished. He slipped down from the stage, crossed to Augie's table, and gathered his friend in an embrace.

Ondrasik donated his entire fee to Augie's Quest and, in so doing, put the night's take at just over two million dollars. When combined with the funds raised at the 2005 lifetime achievement event and the 2006 Bash in Las Vegas, the total money raised by the fitness industry (with a big assist from Lynne's parents) slightly exceeded six million dollars. The total as of June 2007 stood at ten million dollars.

Measured as a philanthropic outpouring from, essentially, one industry for a solitary disease, the amount is little short of staggering. As a tribute to Augie's stature among his colleagues and competitors, it's purely remarkable.

For Augie, though, the funds his foundation raises through events like the annual Bash, through regional celebrity golf outings, and through smaller fund-raising gatherings throughout California and across the nation constitute but half of the equation. Accumulating piles of money is helpful only to the extent that each dollar is well spent, and it is between fund-raisers where Augie's deep talents as an entrepreneur take hold.

There is a reason Augie's friends and colleagues, all canny businesspeople with numerous demands on their resources, remain willing to invest sizeable chunks of their cash in Augie's foundation. Sympathy alone would hardly have carried Augie's Quest this far. Augie's associates are investing in Augie, who knows not just how to raise funds, but precisely how to spend them.

ALEX CAPELLO—friend of the Nietos and fellow YPOer:

My nine-year-old daughter, Sofia, wanted to write a story about Augie, so one afternoon my wife drove her to Augie and Lynne's house, where she interviewed him. Sofia came home a changed person. The transformation was stunning. It was like she'd matured five years in a day.

Sofia told me how special Augie was and how he had changed her heart. "Augie," she said, "will save us all."

CHRIS CLAWSON—former Life Fitness employee and current president of Matrix Fitness:

They might call it Lou Gehrig's disease, but they're going to call it Augie's cure.

You Have Sixty Seconds

———◆———

THE ALS THERAPY Development Institute is located in a quiet corner of Cambridge. The facility occupies eighteen thousand square feet of a refitted nineteenth-century warehouse just a block from the Charles River. There is little that's grand about the space. The administrative side of the operation—the dowdy offices, the common rooms, the carpeted corridors—exude all the charm and cachet of a midmarket radio station, where the glamour and sheen are confined to the studio. The institute sinks its money into its specialists and its cutting-edge equipment.

Among the staff are neuropharmacologists, veterinarians, geneticists, biologists, chemists, surgeons, and assorted general technicians. Once Augie had successfully lured Steve Perrin from Biogen Idec to run the institute's laboratory, Perrin set about equipping the lab and hiring additional scientists for the institute's ambitious assault on ALS. Every aspect of Sean Scott and Sharon Hesterlee's ALS Manhattan Project that can't be economically farmed out to other companies will be conducted in-house, which means an ongoing refit of the institute's lab.

The catalog of equipment and expertise necessary to the project will be monumentally expensive, and that's where Augie comes in. His job as chairman of the board of TDI is to make it possible for Sean, Perrin, and their associates to concentrate on the science alone. Augie will worry about the money.

A quick tour of the TDI facilities is sure to leave even the most benighted layman with a sharpened sense of just how acutely Augie will need to worry. The place is awash in the tools of target discovery and pharmacology; high-end microscopes capable of three-dimensional imaging are set next to others capable of cutting out a single cell for analysis. Infrared scanners are used for protein analysis, and large robotic devices that perform polymerase chain reactions are set up to handle the quantification of RNA. A room full of servers will store the one billion data points that will be generated in the next twelve months.

And then there are the mice. Segregated from the lab and the offices behind an airlock is the institute's mouse facility, the largest ALS mouse lab in the world, housing around fifteen hundred animals at any given time. Animal care is governed by the Institutional Animal Care and Use Committee as well as state and federal regulations enforced by local inspectors. There are also rigorous guidelines for everything from air quality to sanitation. So the filters and air exchangers in the mouse lab ensure a pure and highly ionized atmosphere utterly devoid of the scantest hint of eau de vermin.

Hundreds of SOD1 mice occupy individual plastic habitats shelved throughout the lab. Drugs can be delivered through a variety of routes that are changed from study to study depending on the drug. Some drugs don't mix well with water, some don't like oil, and so on. Simply getting drugs into mice is a science of its own.

The institute's drug studies are ongoing, though the pharmaceutical targets have been largely exhausted in the course of seven years of mouse studies at TDI. The ALS Manhattan Project, with its emphasis on target development, will soon remedy that. To date, the tens of thousands of SOD1 mice that have passed through TDI's facility have served to demonstrate the inefficacy of the full catalog of worldwide pharmaceutical compounds in fighting sporadic ALS. The work has been precise, exhaustive, and, at almost every turn, disappointing.

◆　◆　◆

ON A MONDAY afternoon in May of 2007, the board of directors of the ALS Therapy Development Institute gathered for one of its quarterly meetings. The previous week, Augie had submitted to Dr. Ray Onders's diaphragm pacing surgery in Cleveland, and he'd flown to Boston still sore from the incisions in his muscle wall. As chairman of the board, Augie would conduct the proceedings, and he arrived at the institute in remarkably robust spirits for a man with surgery and an overnight hospital stay only days behind him.

Before the meeting began, the board gathered informally for lunch in the TDI offices with the staff. The meal consisted of burritos and more burritos, Augie's favorite food on the planet. The casual lunch provided an occasion for a few of the newer board members to chat with

the old hands. Once Augie had assumed the chairmanship, shortly after his alliance with the MDA, he'd nomi-
nated several candidates to the board.

They were entrepreneurs and experienced nonprofit
professionals brought on to leaven a board heavy with
Jamie Heywood's family acquaintances, mostly long-
standing Boston business figures. Augie's burrito fest
was intended as an icebreaker, and functioned accord-
ingly since it's hard to be stuffy and aloof with gua-
camole dribbling down your chin.

The board meeting proper convened promptly at one
o'clock in a ground floor conference room. The gathering place was part of the common reception area. Sleek
and urban in design, with a wealth of glass and chrome
and black lacquer, the elegance of the conference space
was very much at odds with the burrito-friendly frumpi-
ness of the institute's upstairs offices. Augie claimed the
head of the table with his wife at his side, and the dozen
board members in attendance filled the other chairs to
capacity. Three additional board members joined by conference call from the West Coast.

Augie opened the meeting by inviting the new members
of the board to introduce themselves. They were pharmaceutical executives, fund managers, attorneys, a former

Watertown High School principal, Jamie Heywood's father, neurologist Stanley Appel of Houston's Methodist Hospital, a portfolio manager, a developmental biologist, and a former special assistant at the Department of Health and Human Services.

It was an impressive bunch, and they shared among them, almost without exception, personal familiarity with the suffering and slow degeneration brought on by ALS. There were stricken spouses, parents, children, aunts, uncles, dear friends. The investment in the cause among the group, the implicit demand for a cure, was intense and abiding.

After the round of introductions, Augie turned his attention to the institute's mission statement. He informed anyone with objections to TDI's explicit mission, "There's the door."

Augie began with the declaration that TDI's goal was "to discover, develop, and deliver promising drugs for treating ALS." He then went on to say, "We envision a center where research science is reconnected to patients by bringing together patients, doctors, and researchers to openly share their findings, knowledge, and insight, and where that information is made available to the world.

We envision a future where this model has expanded and changed the health care system into one that strives and succeeds at effectively seeking treatment for all diseases."

Augie allowed a polite interval for escape, but no one bolted for the door.

He then proceeded with his own gloss on TDI's mission statement. "Our goal is to play two roles," he began. "The first role is the architect. The second role is the general contractor. We don't purport that we can do it all within these four walls. What we do intend is to develop the plan and then diligently follow the practices of a general contractor and hold our subs accountable." Augie continued, "The speed with which we can move when we don't have the brick and mortar to weigh us down will allow us to execute faster, more precisely, and leverage the existing scientific capacity out there that is looking to be led."

Augie paused here for effect and emphasis. ALS might have weakened his voice, but his keen sense of the import and drama of the moment remained unimpaired. "We're the leaders," he said. "We're the architects. Our value is that we're not constrained by traditional thought. We have one goal, and our goal is to find a target we can shoot for. Based upon my assessment, we have the best

chance to do that with our plan." Here Augie was refer-
ring to the sixty-million-dollar ALS Manhattan Project.
"Is there anyone at the table or on the phone who has a
different goal?" he asked.

Again Augie allowed a polite interval for dissent before continuing. "When we start to deviate from our mission, each of you has the responsibility to make sure we
get back on track," he told the board. "It is incredibly seductive to play in a larger arena. What we have chosen to
do is show that people will follow our strategy and our
efforts and will be able to apply them."

Presentations to the board followed, and they began
with the introduction of the new chief financial officer,
Maureen Lister, whose presence on the staff served as a
tacit acknowledgment of the surging fiscal health of the
institute, thanks to the investment made by Augie and the
MDA. Jamie Heywood's overtures to the Pentagon had
also begun paying dividends in recent months. The Department of Defense had been made aware, over the past
few years, of the increased incidence of ALS among service members, particularly among veterans of the Gulf
War. The military incidence of ALS is twice that of the
civilian population, which either sounds alarming or benign, depending on how the figures are presented. "Twice

the incidence" sounds scary. "Two cases in one hundred thousand people rather than one case" seems a bit less alarming.

A presentation on the scientific plan for attacking ALS immediately followed the financial one and promised to be a layman's migraine, given the complexity of ALS and the sophistication of the institute's proposed assault. Sean softened the way for chief science officer Steve Perrin by offering a generally digestible description of what is, at bottom, rather impenetrable science.

"At the end of the day," Sean began, "all disease research starts with 'What's different?' and how that difference causes disease. Next you have to decide if you want to study the problem or find a drug." This is the point where the TDI approach to research departs fundamentally from the academic model. The guiding philosophy of TDI is to leave the "how" for later and concentrate on the "what." "We think that step is important," Sean explained, "but it's already being well funded by the NIH and others."

With a smaller-scale challenge than ALS, this variation in approach would be trivial. "The problem," Sean continued, "is that we're up against fifty-five thousand human genes, forty-two thousand mouse genes, one million proteins, twenty thousand potential viruses in humans, and five hundred kinases [a type of enzyme]."

"We don't want to be beholden to legacy-style investigation when we can now pull this stuff apart massively parallel," Sean said. "The kind of work that used to take a warehouse full of sequencers for the Human Genome Project can now be conducted by a single chip you can hold in your hand."

By Sean's calculation, the sixty-million-dollar ALS discovery effort the institute was embarking upon would result in 1.1 billion data points. "The answer to the question of what stops ALS will be in there," Sean insisted. Clearly, the trick will reside in sifting through the data to find it. "Generating a giant list is of no value if you can't narrow it down," Sean said. "This plan will live or die on our ability to switch on or silence these targets we discover."

Presentations to the board earlier in the proceedings were subject to Augie's sharp stick. If the talk unspooled too slowly and the presenter became enamored of his own voice, Augie was sure to bark, "You have sixty seconds," and mean it. But regardless of the depth of the neurological weeds Sean waded into, there was no danger now of any grumbling from Augie. Given the personal experience with ALS common to the board members, the meeting had an air of dignified urgency, and with Sean and Steve Perrin, the board knew it had arrived at the meat of the matter.

When Sean yielded the floor to Perrin, general scientific principles gave way to thorny biogenetic specifics. Perrin came to the neurogenetic puzzle of ALS with two decades of experience in molecular profiling in both genomics and proteomics. A biochemist by training, he is a translational researcher of the first order, with much hands-on experience in the intricacies of microarray technology. Perrin offered to the board, via a laptop projector, a flowchart devoted to the proposed course of inquiry in the coming months that, for the purposes of the laymen in the group, might as well have been composed in Sanskrit.

The few medically and biochemically trained board members made intermittent inquiries of Perrin and requested the odd explanation while everybody else, mired in relative microbiological ignorance, drew consolation from the fact that his command of the project at hand was comprehensive, even inspired.

At the head of the table, Augie observed the presentation without comment. He lapsed occasionally into the sorts of coughing fits common to ALS patients, the violent and persistent result of an ever-weakening diaphragm. The mere fact of Augie's presiding presence at the ALS Therapy Development Institute's quarterly board meeting was remarkable given the troubled pilgrimage he'd made from the executive suite at Life Fitness, through an ALS diagnosis and a nearly suicidal depression, to a fund-raising alliance with the Muscular Dystrophy Association, and finally to a steering hand in the most ambitious privately-funded assault on human disease ever mounted.

The institute's ALS Manhattan Project might have only been christened at that May meeting, but a more general and fundamental question, long open, had been answered in full.

Who's in charge of curing ALS? Augie is.

◆   ◆   ◆

IN THE FIRST month out of the gate, Steve Perrin, Sean Scott, and company at the ALS Therapy Development Institute completed the largest molecular profiling study ever done on the ALS mouse model. The study was designed to register every change in every gene from the onset of the disease to death. Forty-two thousand genes were tracked every ten days. Clusters of high-powered computer processors continue to churn relentlessly in an effort to divine patterns in the data.

Next up are human samples from the spinal cord, muscle, and blood of ALS patients. The data from the mouse samples and the human samples will be overlaid to determine which genes, if any, are commonly affected by the disease. "Those are ones we'll chase," Sean said.

Newly formed teams at the institute are charged with integrating state-of-the-art neuropharmacology with molecular biology. "We're pushing the envelope here," Perrin allowed. "We're surveying every relevant technology to see what can be turned into an assembly line, everything from gene therapy to drugs." The goal of the project is to narrow the list of candidates using tissues from humans, and multiple mouse lines that get different forms of an ALS-like disease.

Sean, a veteran of hundreds of these mouse studies, added a bit of cautionary perspective. "We're well on our way," he insisted, "but nothing comes easy with this disease."

Inspired by Augie's example, the president of the Muscular Dystrophy Association has recently recommended a comprehensive review of the MDA's research program. The goal is to ensure the organization is funding medical research across its full range of supported diseases as effectively as possible. As effectively, that is to say, as Augie's Quest.

AUGIE:

Two weeks ago, we had a knock at the front door. Claudia, our housekeeper, answered it. It was a realtor, and he asked her if the house was for sale. He told her he'd heard the owner had died.

LYNNE:

Looking out the windows here is almost like watching a live painting. If the ocean means anything to you, this is the place. It's soothing. Beautiful.

AUGIE:

I love this house. I wake up each morning and have the luxury of a home I could never have imagined as a kid.

Early on, right after my diagnosis, I told Lynne this was where I wanted to die. Now it's where I want to live.

In the Cockpit

———◆———

THE PREVAILING RHYTHM of Augie and Lynne Nieto's house is the rhythm of the sea. On every floor, in every room, the sound of breaking waves is inescapable, and the reliable thunder and hiss of the Pacific surf seems to have a hypnotic, sedative effect upon visitors. Friends and associates might come to see Augie on one pressing matter or another, but they invariably end up parked on the terrace or transfixed before a salt-streaked window.

The view is of Catalina Island, twenty-six miles off the coast. Gulls cry, waves pound, cares and obligations fall away. Only Augie presses on with unchecked purpose and confounding goodwill.

Augie operates in what he calls his cockpit, an area just off the kitchen crowded with computer and teleconferencing equipment. There's an oversized trackball on the floor that Augie manipulates by foot with splendid dexterity. Using word-prediction software, he boasts that he can now type forty words a minute. The phone rings dozens of times an hour, and the calls are fielded by Augie's personal assistant, Dahlia. She is Augie's aide, his practical nurse, his foil.

Dahlia is English, lovely, and, if anything, more cheerful than Augie. He calls her Sunshine. Dahlia attended nursing school in Britain but had most recently worked in management at MCI before hearing from a friend of Lynne's that Augie needed an assistant. When Dahlia showed up unarmed with a resume, Augie—ever the stickler—told Lynne he wouldn't see her. A quarter hour later, he'd hired her on the spot.

When asked to compare MCI management with Augie management, Dahlia smiles. "This," she says, "is completely different."

Dahlia forces vitamins on Augie, sneaking in the fish

oil capsules he detests. She feeds him his cherished burritos and punctuates his grousing. They talk and laugh and quarrel and chafe as, together, they do Augie's business.

And Augie's business remains considerable, partly in spite of his disease and partly because of it. Augie has retired from Life Fitness but mantains a position as the company chairman of Octane Fitness, a Minnesota-based equipment manufacturer, and he actively serves on the operating advisory board of North Castle Partners, a Greenwich, Connecticut, investment group. His days, however, are dominated by the demands of being the go-to guy on all things ALS.

Augie and Dahlia answer an unremitting stream of e-mails from well-wishers and fellow patients inspired by Augie's creativity in pushing for a cure for the disease. Fund-raisers, large and small, are always on the horizon, and the MDA's Shannon Shryne regularly makes the drive from her office in San Diego to spend days huddled with Augie over the intricate business of bankrolling a major research effort.

Dahlia and Lynne are oftentimes obliged to gang up on Augie to persuade him to eat, to rest, to take his medications, his vitamins, his antioxidants, his lipoic acid, his fish oil pills. The strain of Augie's schedule—which includes organizing fund-raisers, solving institute problems, and honoring speaking commitments—would be enough to try a healthy man. That Augie can charge ahead full bore two years into an ALS diagnosis is a source of wonder to his colleagues, his doctors, his friends.

Every three months, Augie is evaluated by his neurologist, a man Augie fondly refers to as "my nerdy Pakistani doctor." Forty-two-year-old Tahseen Mozaffar presides over a spanking new clinic for which Augie's Quest provided a half million dollars in seed money. The University of California at Irvine's ALS and Neuromuscular Center is an MDA-sponsored state-of-the-art facility and home to Augie's team, as he calls them.

Physical therapist Sandhya Rao, whom Augie refers to as his quarterback, is regularly in and out of Augie and Lynne's home seeing to Augie's comfort and fine-tuning the equipment needed to keep him operating at his customary breakneck pace. The clinic's director of rehab services, Mahendra Shah, functions as Augie's unofficial spiritual advisor. Mahendra gives off an air of serenity as if it were cologne.

"We are here," Mahendra says, "to help our patients on

their journey." When Augie now insists, as he frequently does, that he is "redefining normal every day," he is merely paraphrasing Mahendra Shah.

Dr. Mozaffar and Augie are given to jousting over treatment options. Thanks chiefly to the Internet, most ALS patients stay scrupulously informed about new drugs and therapies. As chairman of the board of an ALS laboratory and with access, through the MDA, to the nation's leading neurologists, Augie is in a universe by himself when it comes to exposure to cutting-edge ALS therapies.

"A lot of times, I'm carrying out orders from somebody else," Dr. Mozaffar allows, "and I may not necessarily agree with them. It becomes a challenge to draw the line."

Augie and Dr. Mozaffar share an enthusiasm for proactive measures. It was Dr. Mozaffar who recommended the diaphragm pacing system, and he impresses as a man sufficiently secure in his expertise to not merely tolerate suggestions on treatment but even invite them. Consequently, Dr. Mozaffar has jousted not just with Augie but with Sean Scott as well. "I love Sean, but you can't win an argument with him," Dr. Mozaffar says, laughing. "He has a rhetoric degree. It's hopeless."

The fondness Augie and his team share among them is

palpable and conspicuous. They are surely helping each other on their journeys.

There is widespread agreement among the people who know Augie that if anybody can orchestrate and engineer a cure for a disease as fiendishly challenging as ALS, he's the guy. Until that day, Augie continues to prove minute by minute and hour by hour that even though his body may betray him, his abundance of grace and compassion never will.

Augie's cell phone vibrates with calls throughout each day. He wears a Bluetooth earpiece and rolls himself around in his cockpit chair as he talks to associates and colleagues, friends and relative strangers. Invariably, they ask him how he's doing.

Just as invariably, and with infectious high spirits, Augie tells them, "I'm great!"

Acknowledgments

My wife, Lynne, and our children—Nicole, Danielle, Austin, and Lindsay—have been a constant source of inspiration for me. I can hardly imagine their despair in watching their husband and father battle ALS while knowing the chance of a timely cure is slim. I am grateful to know what unconditional, nonjudgmental love feels like.

I would like to thank my brother-in-law, Dr. Kent Bransford, for his patience and expertise, and Lynne's parents, Jack and Kathy Bransford, for their extraordinary support of our cause. No son-in-law could be prouder.

Our drive to defeat ALS couldn't possibly have a better partner than the Muscular Dystrophy Association. My thanks go out to CEO Jerry Weinberg, Sharon Hesterlee, vice president of translational research, and Shannon Shryne, fund-raiser extraordinaire, along with everyone else at the MDA who has worked to make Augie's Quest a Goliath in the battle against ALS.

I would also like to thank my friends and colleagues at the ALS Therapy Development Institute: Sean Scott, whom I trust with not just my life but the lives of all ALS sufferers, chief scientific officer Steve Perrin, and Jamie Heywood, our organization's founding force.

Thank you to Dr. Tahseen Mozaffar for the insight and advice that make my journey with ALS tolerable. And deep, abiding thanks to Augie's Angels: my physical therapist and quarterback, Sandhya Rao, and my personal assistant, Dahlia. She's not just my right hand but my left hand as well, since I can no longer use either.

A special thanks to our family and friends . . . "the ones who show up!" . . . and to everyone who has joined the battle against ALS by donating to Augie's Quest. I'd like to express my personal gratitude to Mitch Albom, who passed along to me the magical lesson Morrie Schwartz taught him: one life touches another . . . which touches another . . . which touches another.

Finally, Tom Pearson and I would like to thank our

agent, David Black, for his enthusiasm and guidance, along with editor Kathy Belden and publisher Karen Rinaldi at Bloomsbury. We are grateful for their invaluable advice and hard work.

A Note on the Authors

AUGIE NIETO popularized the Lifecycle and has been a leader in the fitness industry for nearly three decades. He is the cofounder and former president of Life Fitness and is now chairman of Octane Fitness. Augie is cochair, with his wife, Lynne, of the Muscular Dystrophy Association's ALS Division. He's the father of four children, and he and Lynne live in Corona del Mar, California.

T. R. PEARSON has written ten novels, one work of nonfiction, and six screenplays. He lives in Greenwood, Virginia.